Construction Dispute Review Board Manual

Construction Dispute Review Board Manual

Robert M. Matyas

A. A. Mathews, P.E.

Robert J. Smith, P.E., Esq.

P. E. Sperry, P.E.

McGraw-Hill

New York   San Francisco   Washington, D.C.   Auckland   Bogotá
Caracas   Lisbon   London   Madrid   Mexico City   Milan
Montreal   New Delhi   San Juan   Singapore
Sydney   Tokyo   Toronto

Library of Congress Cataloging-in-Publication Data

Construction dispute review board manual / Robert M. Matyas ... [et
al.].
        p.   cm.
    Includes bibliographical references and index.
    ISBN 0-07-041060-7 (hc)
    1. Construction contracts—United States. 2. Dispute resolution
(Law)—United States. I. Matyas, Robert M.
    KF902.C614   1995
    343.73'078624—dc20
    [347.30378624]   95-32923
                                                          CIP

McGraw-Hill

A Division of The McGraw·Hill Companies

    3 4 5 6 7 8 9 0   DOC/DOC   9 0 0 9

ISBN 0-07-041060-7

*The sponsoring editor for this book was Larry Hager, the editing supervisor
was Jane Palmieri, and the production supervisor was Suzanne W. B.
Rapcavage. It was set in Palatino by Estelita F. Green of McGraw-Hill's
Professional Book Group composition unit.*

Printed and bound by R. R. Donnelley & Sons Company.

McGraw-Hill books are available at special quantity discounts to use as
premiums and sales promotions, or for use in corporate training pro-
grams. For more information, please write to the Director of Special
Sales, McGraw-Hill, 11 West 19th Street, New York, NY 10011. Or
contact your local bookstore.

This book is printed on recycled, acid-free paper containing a
minimum of 50% recycled, de-inked fiber.

Contents

3. International Applications   63

Series Introduction

Construction is America's largest manufacturing industry. Ahead of automotive and chemicals, it represents 14 percent of this country's gross national product. Yet construction is unique in that it is the only manufacturing industry in which the factory goes out to the point of sale. Every end product has a life of its own and is different from all others, although component parts may be mass-produced, or modular.

Because of this uniqueness, the construction industry needs and deserves a literature of its own, beyond reworked civil engineering texts and trade publication articles.

Whether the topic is management methods, business briefings, or field technology, it is covered professionally and progressively in this series. The working contractor aspires to deliver to the owner a superior product that is ahead of schedule, under budget, and out of court. This series, written by constructors for constructors, is dedicated to that goal.

M. D. Morris, P.E.
Series Editor

Preface

The number and magnitude of disputes between contractors and owners continues to be a serious problem in the construction industry. Disputes result in a substantial dilution of effort, delays, and diversion of capital.

Considerable progress to alleviate the problem has been made in many fields of construction. The progress has primarily taken the form of more equitable allocation of risk between the contractor and the owner coupled with use of alternative dispute resolution (ADR) procedures. ADR has many forms, most of which are employed (as in litigation) after the work has been completed. The decisions are sometimes made by people who have limited background in the type of work involved and no firsthand familiarity with the specific project.

An ADR procedure that can provide early attention to disputes arising during contract performance is the dispute review board (DRB). This manual describes how a DRB helps settle disputes during construction. Further, it defines the process of writing a DRB into a construction contract and the subsequent operation of a board. Included are case studies, guide documents for implementation of a board, and a tabulation of projects utilizing the system.

A DRB consists of three members, all selected jointly by the contractor and the owner, who are experienced with the type of work involved, are respected by their peers, and approach their responsibilities with complete neutrality and impartiality. Their involvement is contemporaneous; they regularly receive construction progress reports, meet with the parties, and tour the job site.

Experience has shown that the mere existence of a DRB minimizes the outbreak of disputes. When conflicts do arise, the DRB is able to recommend settlement quickly, before adversarial attitudes escalate to the extent that construction cost and schedule are compromised. The cost of the DRB—estimated at 0.1 to 0.3 percent of construction costs—is very small compared with the cost of possible litigation.

The performance record of DRBs is impressive. It is recommended that a DRB be provided for all construction projects on which substantial disputes could arise. DRBs have been successfully utilized on projects costing as little as $7 million. Over 300 disputes have been heard and resolved on almost 200 projects worth over $10 billion. To date, no courtroom adjudication is known to have resulted from DRB projects.

Acknowledgments

To the following people, the authors express their appreciation for written contributions and opinions, pertinent experiences, discussions, and moral support during the preparation of this manual.

Mr. Romano Allione	Impregilo, Spa	Milano, Italy
Harry L. Arkin, Esq.	Harry L. Arkin & Associates	Denver, CO
Dr. Ing. Gianni A. Arrigoni	Societa Italiana Gallerie	Carimate, Italy
Prof. S. H. Bartholomew	Chico State University	Chico, CA
Dr. Gary S. Brierley	Haley & Aldrich, Inc.	Cambridge, MA
Mr. Eugene F. Casey	Construction engineer	Brooklyn, NY
Mr. Michael Cate	M-K Ferguson	Cleveland, OH
Mr. John D. Coffee	Federal Highway Administration	Olympia, WA

Mr. Hugh E. Cronin	UCIC Consultants	Costa Mesa, CA
Mr. Raymond J. Dodson	Consultant	Woodside, CA
James P. Groton, Esq.	Sutherland, Asbill & Brennan	Atlanta, GA
Dr. Marshall Gysi	FIDIC	Lausanne, Switzerland
Mr. David Hammond	Consultant	Ft. Belvoir, VA
Gordon L. Jaynes, Esq.	Whitman, Breed, Abbot & Morgan	Surrey, England
James Jones, Esq.	U.S. Army Corps of Engineers	Baltimore, MD
Mr. Francis S. Kendorski	Consulting engineer	Downers Grove, IL
Mr. Thomas R. Kuesel	Parsons Brinckerhoff	Charlottes-ville, VA
Mr. Jack K. Lemley	Lemley & Associates, Inc.	Boise, ID
Dr. Ing. Igor V. Leto	Institution of Civil Engineers	Rome, Italy
Mr. Walter Marlowe	ASCE	Washington, DC
Mr. T. M. McDougall	T. M. McDougall Pty., Ltd.	E. Lindfield, Australia
Mr. Norman Nadel	Nadel Associates	Brewster, NY
Mr. Carlos S. Ospina	Ingetec, S.A.	Bogota, Columbia
Theodore J. Ralph, Esq.	Johnston, Ralph, Reed & Watt	San Antonio, TX
Robert A. Rubin, Esq.	Postner & Rubin	New York, NY

Mr. Winfield O. Salter	Parsons Brinckerhoff	Atlanta, GA
Mr. M. Tomei	Impregilo, S.P.A.	Milano, Italy
Dr. Timothy E. Toohig, S.J.	Boston College	Boston, MA
Prof. Mike C. Vorster	Virginia Polytechnic Institute	Blacksburg, VA

These people also prepared and submitted first-draft papers for consideration as chapter topics.

Prof. S. H. Bartholomew	Chico State University	Chico, CA
Dr. Gary S. Brierley	Haley & Aldrich, Inc.	Cambridge, MA
Mr. Michael Cate	M-K Ferguson	Cleveland, OH
Mr. Hugh E. Cronin	UCIC Consultants	Costa Mesa, CA
Mr. Raymond J. Dodson	Consultant	Woodside, CA
James P. Groton, Esq.	Sutherland, Asbill & Brennan	Atlanta, GA
Mr. David Hammond	Consultant	Ft. Belvoir, VA
Gordon L. Jaynes, Esq.	Whitman, Breed, Abbot & Morgan	Surrey, England
James Jones, Esq.	U.S. Army Corps of Engineers	Baltimore, MD
Mr. Thomas R. Kuesel	Parsons Brinckerhoff	Charlottes-ville, VA
Mr. Norman Nadel	Nadel Associates	Brewster, NY
Robert A. Rubin, Esq.	Postner & Rubin	New York, NY

| Prof. Mike C. Vorster | Virginia Polytechnic Institute | Blacksburg, VA |

The authors thank the following reviewers for providing many constructive suggestions on an early draft of the manuscript.

John D. Alkire, Esq.	Perkins Coie	Seattle, WA
Mr. Romano Allione	Impregilo, Spa	Milano, Italy
Harry L. Arkin, Esq.	Harry L. Arkin & Associates	Denver, CO
Dr. Ing. Gianni A. Arrigoni	Societa Italiana Gallerie	Carimate, Italy
Mr. James Ball	Delcan-Hatch	Toronto, Ontario, Canada
Ralph R. Barnard, Esq.	Barnard & Brown	Lansing, NY
Prof. S. H. Bartholomew	Chico State University	Chico, CA
John E. Beard III, Esq.	Kirkpatrick & Lockhart	Pittsburgh, PA
Ms. Bethany J. Berridge	Wickwire Gavin PC	Madison, WI
Gabriel L. I. Bevilacqua, Esq.	Saul Ewing, Remick & Saul	Philadelphia, PA
Mr. Brian Bowers	KFC Airport, Incorporated	Honolulu, HI
Dr. Gary S. Brierley	Haley & Aldrich, Inc.	Cambridge, MA
Frank Carr, Esq.	U.S. Army Corps of Engineers	Washington, DC
Mr. Eugene F. Casey	Construction engineer	Brooklyn, NY
Mr. Hugh P. Caspe	Sverdrup Civil, Inc.	Boston, MA
Mr. Michael Cate	M-K Ferguson	Cleveland, OH

Mr. Charles Cimino, AIA	Boston Society of Architects	Boston, MA
Peter H. J. Chapman, Esq.	Peter Chapman Consultants	Surrey, England
Mr. John D. Coffee	Federal Highway Administration	Olympia, WA
Mr. Edward Cohen	Ammann & Whitney	New York, NY
Prof. Edward J. Cording	University of Illinois	Savoy, IL
Mr. Hugh E. Cronin	UCIC Consultants	Costa Mesa, CA
Mr. Richard Curl	Balfour Beatty, Ltd.	Miami, FL
Sharon F. Daily, Esq.	Greensfelder Hemkerale Gale	St. Louis, MO
Mr. Robert Del Re	Consultant	Tampa, FL
Mr. Frank Delle Cave	Ingersoll-Rand	Ridgewood, NJ
Mr. Ray A. Dipasquale, R.A.	Ray A. Dipasquale Associates	Ithaca, NY
Mr. Raymond J. Dodson	Consultant	Woodside, CA
Mr. Peter M. Douglass	Consultant	Seattle, WA
Mr. Paul Eller	Eller Associates	Soquel, CA
Mr. E. Harvey Elwin	Bechtel	Randle, WA
Mr. Randall J. Essex	Woodward-Clyde	Oakland, CA
Michael Feigen, Esq.	Lehrer McGovern Bovis, Inc.	New York, NY
Mr. George Freidman	American Arbitration Association	Washington, DC
Mr. Sven-Erik Frick-Meijer	International Construction	Stockholm, Sweden

Mr. Vernon K. Garrett, Jr.	Delon Hampton & Associates	Washington, DC
Mr. Paul Gilbert	Parsons Brinckerhoff	Seattle, WA
Mr. Donald R. Goodkind	Engineering consultant	Pacific Palisades, CA
James P. Groton, Esq.	Sutherland, Asbill & Brennan	Atlanta, GA
Mr. Joseph D. Guertin, Jr.	GZA Geo-Environmental, Inc.	Newton Upper Falls, MA
Dr. Albert H. Halff	Albert Halff Associates	Dallas, TX
Mr. David Hammond	Consultant	Ft. Belvoir, VA
Mr. Oliver T. Harding	HNTB	Layton, UT
Mr. Michael D. Heath, AIA	Heath Associates	Melrose, MA
Mr. Paul Heather	Mare Associates	Bellevue, WA
Dr. Ronald E. Heuer	Geotechnical consultant	McHenry, IL
Mr. John Hickey, Jr.	Pennsylvania Turnpike Commission	Harrisburg, PA
Mr. H. Murray Hohns	H. Murray Hohns, Inc.	Honolulu, HI
Mr. David E. Holland	Private consultant	Auckland, New Zealand
Prof. Tom Iseley	Louisiana Tech University	Ruston, LA
Gordon L. Jaynes, Esq.	Whitman, Breed, Abbot & Morgan	Surrey, England

Mr. Douglas Johnson	Al Johnson Construction Co.	Minneapolis, MN
Maj. Gen. James A. Johnson	U. S. Army Corps of Engineers (ret.)	Fairfax Station, VA
Mr. Don Jones	Hyman Construction	San Francisco, CA
James Jones, Esq.	U.S. Army Corps of Engineers	Baltimore, MD
Christopher Kane, Esq.	Lyon & McManus	Washington, DC
Mr. J. M. Keating	Keating Associates	Placerville, CA
Mr. Martin N. Kelley	Kiewit Construction Group, Inc.	Omaha, NB
Mr. Francis S. Kendorski	Consulting engineer	Downers Grove, IL
Mr. Vladimir Khazak	O'Brien-Kreitzberg Associates	Seattle, WA
Mr. Gail B. Knight	Tunnel consultant	Frankfort, IL
Mr. Joe Kracum	DMJM	Glenwood Springs, CO
Mr. Thomas R. Kuesel	Parsons Brinckerhoff	Charlottes-ville, VA
Mr. Merle E. Larrabee	Caltrans	Sacramento, CA
Dr. Ing. Igor V. Leto	Institution of Civil Engineers	Rome, Italy
Mr. Richard A. Lewis	Granite Construction	Watsonville, CA
Mr. Philip C. Loots	Philip Loots Associates	Benmore, South Africa
Mr. Tracy Lundin	Sverdrup Civil, Inc.	Boston, MA

Mr. John F. MacDonald	Atkinson Construction Co.	Enumclaw, WA
Ms. Kathleen K. Mayo	BART	Oakland, CA
Mr. Dennis McCarry	Consultant	Gilroy, CA
Mr. Terry McCusker	Tunnel consultant	San Francisco, CA
Mr. T. M. McDougall	T. M. McDougall Pty., Ltd.	E. Lindfield, Australia
Mr. Russell K. McFarland	Nuclear Waste Technical Review Board	Alexandria, VA
James McVety, Esq.	Hancock, Estabrook	Syracuse, NY
Mr. James Meinholz	Consultant	Wautoma, WI
Ms. Marjorie Meyer	A. A. Mathews Corporation	Federal Way, WA
Mr. Gary Miller	Cannon	Grand Island, NY
James C . Moore, Esq.	Harter, Secrest & Emory	Rochester, NY
Mr. George Morschauser	Parsons-Dillingham	Los Angeles, CA
James J. Meyers, Esq.	Gadsby & Hannah	Boston, MA
Mr. Norman Nadel	Nadel Associates	Brewster, NY
Mr. Jerome C. Neyer	NTH Consultants, Ltd.	Farmington Hills, MI
Mr. K. B. Norris	Sir Alexander Gibbs & Partners	Berkshire, England
Mr. Carlos S. Ospina	Ingetec, S.A.	Bogota, Columbia

Mr. Edward W. Peterson	Construction consultant	Bodega Bay, CA
Mr. A. M. Petrofsky	Jacobs Associates	San Francisco, CA
Theodore J. Ralph, Esq.	Johnston, Ralph, Reed & Watt	San Antonio, TX
Mr. Stephen G. Revay	Revay & Associates, Limited	Montreal, Quebec, Canada
Robert A. Rubin, Esq.	Postner & Rubin	New York, NY
Mr. Winfield O. Salter	Parsons Brinckerhoff	Atlanta, GA
Mr. Rube Samuels	Parsons Brinckerhoff	New York, NY
Mr. Karl F. Schmid	Baruch College	New York, NY
Mr. Birger Schmidt	Parsons Brinckerhoff	San Francisco, CA
Mr. Mike Shanley	Consultant	Novato, CA
Neal R. Stamp, Esq.	Cornell University (ret.)	Ithaca, NY
Mr. Ken Stinson	Kiewit Construction Group, Inc.	Omaha, NE
Mr. William F. Swiger	Consulting engineer	Buhl, ID
Dr. Peter Tarkoy	GeoConSol, Inc.	Medfield, MA
Dr. Timothy Toohig, S.J.	Boston College	Boston, MA
Mr. Ralph J. Trapani	Colorado Division of Highways	Glenwood Springs, CO

Thomas Treacy, Esq.	Buckley, Treacy, Schaffel, Mackey & Abbate	New York, NY
Prof. Mike C. Vorster	Virginia Polytechnic Institute	Blacksburg, VA
Mr. Christian H. Walser	The World Bank	Washington, DC

Predecessor Efforts

In 1989, the publication *Avoiding and Resolving Disputes in Underground Construction* was published by the American Society of Civil Engineers. A revision followed in 1991 titled *Avoiding and Resolving Disputes During Construction*. These works were prepared by the Underground Technology Research Council (UTRC), sponsored by committees of the American Society of Civil Engineers and the American Institute of Mining, Metallurgical, and Petroleum Engineers.

The Technical Committee on Contracting Practices of the Underground Technology Research Council
1987 to 1990

Peter M. Douglass *chairman* Private consultant Seattle, WA	Renon Hoge Mole Construction Company Solon, OH
Rodney Aschenbrenner Guy F. Atkinson Co. (ret.) Los Altos Hills, CA	Douglas Johnson Al Johnson Construction Co. Minneapolis, MN
Vernon K. Garrett, Jr. Delon Hampton & Associates Washington, DC	A. A. Mathews A. A. Mathews Corporation Federal Way, WA
David Hammond Consulting engineer La Canada, CA	Robert M. Matyas Private consultant Ithaca, NY
William H. Hansmire Kiewet/PB Las Vegas, NV	Kenneth Schoeman Bureau of Reclamation (ret.) Ickewood, CO

Robert J. Smith, Esq.
Wickwire Gavin, P.C.
Madison, WI

P. E. (Joe) Sperry
Tunnel construction consultant
Boulder City, NV

The Technical Committee on
Contracting Practices of the
Underground Technology Research Council
1991

P. E. (Joe) Sperry   *chairman*
Tunnel construction consultant
Boulder City, NV

Frank Carr, Esq.
Chief Trial Attorney
U.S. Army Corps of Engineers
Washington, DC

John D. Coffee
Federal Highway
  Administration
Olympia, WA

Oliver T. Harding
Washington State Department
  of Transportation
Seattle, WA

Ronald E. Heuer
Geotechnical consultant
McHenry, IL

Martin N. Kelley
Vice President, Engineering
  (ret.)
Kiewit Construction Group,
  IDG
Omaha, NB

Vladimir Khazak
Director, Technical Services
Municipality of Metro Seattle
Seattle, WA

John F. MacDonald
Project Manager
Guy F. Atkinson Company
Los Angeles, CA

A. A. Mathews
A. A. Mathews Corporation
Federal Way, WA

Norman A. Nadel
Nadel Associates, Inc.
Brewster, NY

John E. Reeves
Chief, Office of Highway
  Construction
California Department of
  Transportation
Sacramento, CA

Robert A. Rubin, Esq.
Postner & Rubin
New York, NY

Robert J. Smith, Esq.
Wickwire Gavin, P.C.
Madison, WI

Construction
Dispute Review
Board Manual

1
Concept and Experience

1.0 Introduction

1.0.1 Background

The first definitive reference and user's guide on dispute review boards (DRBs) was published in 1989 by the American Society of Civil Engineers (ASCE) under the title *Avoiding and Resolving Disputes in* **Underground Construction.** The guide was updated and revised in 1991 as *Avoiding and Resolving Disputes* **During Construction.** The subject matter and title were expanded to make it clear the concept was not limited to underground construction. Both of these guides contained a narrative description of the process, a suggested specification, and a model three-party agreement.

Also in these publications was a chapter devoted to escrow bid documents (EBDs) for use in facilitating dispute resolution, particularly in negotiating change order pricing. For continuity, these EBD procedures, with some modification, are included as Appendix G of this manual. There was also a chapter recommending that a geotechnical design summary report (GDSR) be included in the contract documents to provide a geotechnical baseline for all anticipated subsurface conditions. This text is being revised and expanded in a separate publication renamed *Geotechnical Reports for Underground Construction,* to be developed under the auspices of the ASCE. That publication will present the rationale for changing GDSR to geotechnical baseline report (GBR). For continuity, Chapter 5 of the 1991 edition is reproduced verbatim (with the recommended term GBR substituted) in Appendix F.

Since 1991, use of DRBs as a means of dispute prevention and resolution has expanded, both geographically and with respect to industry applications. For example, on private projects, highways, and building projects, the recorded DRB usage has tripled. Variations and permutations were created and adopted—some successfully, some not, as described later. The Construction Industry Institute (CII) conducted an extensive, structured study of the DRB process in action. All these factors led to the conclusion that the industry could benefit from an expanded and updated guide.

1.0.2 Purpose

This publication is intended primarily as a reference and a user's guide. Thus, the title *DRB Manual* was selected. It is directed toward owners, construction managers, architects, engineers, contractors, attorneys, and others who are working with the process as well as toward those contemplating the use of a DRB. It explains the benefits, points out the pitfalls, describes the procedures, and provides guide specifications necessary to employ the DRB process. It is also intended to help users and participants employ the process more effectively.

1.0.3 Approach

This book started with a collection of contributed papers representing the combined experience, observations, and informed opinions of several dozen individuals who have served as DRB members. They represent service on more than 100 dispute review boards, with some contributors going back to the first DRB nearly 20 years ago. Their construction experience ranges from underground and surface civil construction to building and process projects. Additional review comments and suggestions were received from owners, designers, contractors, and attorneys involved with over 120 owner and design professional organizations, contractors, and contracting agencies, both in the United States and abroad. These contributors have been involved in the preparation of numerous DRB specifications and have worked under various kinds of DRB specifications and three-party agreements.

1.0.4 Scope

This manual consists of three major parts: (1) Concept and Experience, (2) Practice, and (3) International Applications. We discuss the DRB concept in Sections 1.0 to 1.7. Section 1.1 opens with an overview of the DRB process, followed by a history of its use in Section 1.2. Those elements of the process that are deemed essential are explained and evaluated in Section 1.3. The benefits of the DRB process are addressed in Section 1.4. In Section 1.5, some of the perceived barriers are identified and critiqued. Section 1.6 lists and comments on several variations of the process. We discuss the perceptions and perspectives of all participants in Section 1.7. Practice is covered in Sections 2.0 and 2.4. Finally, applications outside the United States, where DRB use is expanding, are described in Sections 3.0 to 3.3.

Reference material for this manual is found in the appendixes. An updated tabulation of the known uses of DRBs appears in Appendix A, followed by selected case histories in Appendix B. The recommended DRB specification and three-party agreement are presented in Appendix C. They incorporate minor revisions to the suggested specification and agreement that appeared in earlier editions. Also included are a sample format for DRB recommendations (Appendix D) and examples of such recommendations (Appendix E). The 1991 geotechnical baseline report (GBR) procedures are presented in Appendix F, and the escrow bid document (EBD) concept is described in Appendix G.

1.1 Summary Description of the DRB

1.1.1 Overview—A Method for Avoiding and Resolving Disputes at the Job Site

The DRB is a panel of three experienced, respected, and impartial reviewers. The board is organized before construction begins and meets at the job site periodically. DRB members are provided with the contract plans and specifications, become familiar with the project procedures and the participants, and are kept abreast of job progress and developments. The DRB meets with the owner and contractor representatives during regular site visits and encourages the resolution of disputes at the job level.

When any dispute flowing from the contract or the work cannot be resolved by the parties, it is referred to the DRB. The board review includes a hearing at which each party explains its position and answers questions from the other party and the DRB. In arriving at a recommendation, the DRB considers the relevant contract documents, correspondence, other documentation, and the particular circumstances of the dispute.

The board's output consists of a written, nonbinding recommendation for resolution of the dispute. The report normally includes an explanation of the board's evaluation of the facts and contract provisions and the reasoning which led to its conclusions. Acceptance by the parties is facilitated by their confidence in the DRB—in its members' technical expertise, firsthand understanding of the project conditions, and practical judgment—as well as by the parties' opportunity to be heard.

1.1.2 Overview of How a DRB Is Organized

Typically, and often with the recommendation of the designer, the owner decides to provide for a DRB on a project and incorporates the required provisions in the bidding documents. Soon after contract award, each party proposes one member and those two select the third member. The appointments of all three members are subject to approval by both parties. The board is finally established through the execution of a three-party agreement by both parties and the DRB members. Each member is required to serve both owner and contractor with total impartiality.

The DRB typically conducts an initial organizational meeting at the site when construction is just beginning. It meets with both parties and is supplied with copies of the contract documents. A project briefing acquaints the DRB with the nature of

1. Owner evaluates applicability of DRB.
2. Owner decides to use DRB.
3. Owner coordinates DRB provisions with standard contract language and includes DRB specification and three-party agreement in bidding documents.
4. After contract award, each party nominates one DRB member.
5. Contractor and owner each approve other's nominee.
6. Owner provides first two members with contract documents.
7. First two DRB members confer and select third member.
8. Both parties approve third member.
9. Owner provides third member with contract documents.
10. Three-party agreement signed.
11. Organizational meeting held at site.

Figure 1.1. Steps in formation of a DRB.

the work and the contractor's plans for executing it. Procedures and timing for the board's regular site visits are established. The steps in forming a DRB are summarized in Fig. 1.1. All steps should be completed promptly, in accordance with the guide specification. Procrastination in forming the DRB can reduce the effectiveness of the entire procedure.

It should be pointed out that even if the contract does not provide for a DRB, the parties may agree to organize a board after the contract is awarded. This would require only a change order adopting the DRB specification and three-party agreement and making appropriate changes in the original contract. Again, timeliness is advantageous.

1.1.3 Summary of DRB Responsibilities

The DRB has the following principal responsibilities:

1. Visit the site periodically.
2. Keep abreast of job activities and developments.
3. Encourage the resolution of disputes by the parties.

4. When a dispute is referred to it, conduct a hearing, complete its deliberations, and prepare a recommendation in a professional and timely manner.

Details on discharging DRB responsibilities are provided in other sections of this manual.

1.1.4 Costs

The direct costs of the DRB include the fees and expenses of the board members. The time spent by employees of the contracting parties in preparing for and participating in DRB meetings is not a significant burden when reviewed in the light of the time both parties devote to internal claims negotiations and other matters. It is probably comparable to partnering (see Section 1.2.5) in terms of total costs.

The direct DRB costs for periodic site visits and meetings, which usually average about four per year, are easily estimated. Each member's fees typically range from $1000 to $2000 per day. Regular site visits and meetings normally require only one day plus about one day of travel time. Time spent reviewing progress reports and preparing for meetings is usually nominal—perhaps less than one hour per month. The duties of the chairperson will require somewhat more time. Travel and subsistence costs as well as other reimbursable expenses can be estimated with reasonable accuracy. The Construction Industry Institute (CII) characterizes the expense of these regular site visits as prevention costs, yielding the benefit of prevention as a result of the board's presence. Although the value of this benefit cannot be quantified, owners and contractors who have used the DRB process generally agree that the value far exceeds the cost.

The cost of a DRB hearing depends on the time required for the hearing itself as well as the time required by the DRB to deliberate and then prepare its written recommendations. For a simple case, the hearing might be included with a regular site visit and the deliberations and recommendation issued that day or the following day. Complex cases might require several days of hearings and weeks for DRB deliberations and report preparation. Although the cost of resolution cannot be predicted at the beginning of the project, it is certainly far less than the cost of arbitration or litigation. Weighed against the timeliness and effectiveness of this resolution process, the cost compares favorably with that of other alternative dispute resolution (ADR) measures. A review of case histories (see Appendix B) indicates that total direct DRB costs generally are considerably less than 0.5 percent of the final contract price.

1.2 The Development of the DRB Concept

1.2.1 Background

Historical records of the construction industry through the early part of the twentieth century contain little information on the frequency and seriousness of disputes and litigation. Nevertheless, because of the highly individualistic nature of construction projects, disagreements were inevitable. It appears that up until the 1940s, commonly used procedures—such as prompt, informal arbitration or a ruling by the architect or engineer—were generally sufficient to resolve most disputes at the job level.

This state of affairs began to deteriorate after World War II. The postwar period ushered in a tremendous expansion of the construction industry, accompanied by a corresponding growth in transportation and communication facilities. As a result, contractors became more mobile, venturing without hesitation into unfamiliar regions and seeking work from owners who were new to them. As competition became increasingly keen, reduced profit margins were further eroded, particularly during periods of rapid inflation. Contracts became much more complex and the construction process was burdened with nontechnical requirements such as environmental regulations and third-party interventions. Contractors were compelled to pursue all available means to maintain their financial well-being, and a growing body of lawyers and consultants stood ready to accommodate them.

As this deterioration in business climate became more and more evident, the construction industry increasingly sought sensible solutions. Arbitration became more popular, but in many cases it became more formal and more like litigation. Both processes were becoming more expensive, more time-consuming, and less satisfactory. The ensuing movement away from litigation is marked by several events which led up to the DRB concept. Two of these are described below.

1.2.2 Boundary Dam, State of Washington

The Boundary Dam and Underground Powerhouse complex is located about 100 miles north of Spokane, Washington, near the Canadian border. It was constructed in the mid-1960s by Seattle City Light.

As the project approached the critical stage, when the civil work had to be far enough along to allow access for the turbine and generator contractors, the general contractor was behind schedule and in a precarious financial situation. Unsuccessful in pursuing large claims against City Light, the contractor was threatening to curtail the work in order to pressure the owner into action.

At that very time, Seattle City Light was engaged in litigation involving the recently completed raising of Gorge High Dam, north of Seattle. Reluctant to become embroiled in another long legal battle, City Light suggested that each party appoint two people to a four-person "joint consulting board," which would make recommendations regarding conflicts on the job site and contractor's claims. Since Seattle City Light could not legally submit to binding arbitration, the recommendations of the board could be accepted or rejected by either party. Four experienced construction professionals were appointed to the board, which went into action at once. As a result, several administrative procedures on the job were streamlined, relations between the contractor and the owner were improved, and several claims were settled. After the job was completed, all remaining claims were resolved without litigation.

1.2.3 *Better Contracting for Underground Construction*

In 1972, shortly after the organization of the U.S. National Committee on Tunneling Technology, Standing Subcommittee

No. 4 was given the assignment to study contracting practices throughout the world. The objective was to develop recommendations for improved contracting methods in the United States. The subcommittee recognized that contracting practices in the United States were inadequate for current conditions and constituted a serious barrier to the application of new technology and to the containment of rapidly escalating construction costs and contract disputes.

The study included a comprehensive review of contracting practices throughout the world, particularly in Europe. Areas in which U.S. practices appeared to be deficient were identified and subjected to further review and discussions. The study culminated in a 3-day workshop attended by more than 50 individuals representing a cross section of the disciplines involved in the construction industry. The workshop developed specific conclusions and recommendations on 17 different subjects. These were thoroughly described in the report *Better Contracting for Underground Construction*, published in 1974 under the auspices of the U.S. National Academy of Sciences.

It is notable that the *Better Contracting* report frequently dwells on the deleterious effect of claims, disputes, and litigation upon the efficiency of the construction process. Many of the specific recommendations are aimed at mitigating this problem. The last of the 17 recommendations, entitled "Arbitration," explores this subject further. It brings out some of the shortcomings of the arbitration process as then practiced.

Better Contracting was well received in construction industry circles. Over the years, increasing numbers of consulting engineers and owners adopted its recommendations. There is no question that this report exposed many of the problems facing the construction industry and increased awareness of the high cost of claims, disputes, and litigation to the industry and the public.

1.2.4 The First Two Decades

Shortly after publication of *Better Contracting for Underground Construction*, the DRB concept appeared. Although its unique features were recognized and appreciated, the industry was slow to take advantage of the process. However, the success of early uses eventually convinced a growing number of project owners and contractors. The record during the next two decades illustrates the dramatic rise of the DRB, as described in the following sections.

1.2.4.1 1975 to 1985. The first generally recorded use of the DRB concept was applied to the construction contract for the second bore of the Eisenhower Tunnel, in Colorado. Construction of the first bore, between 1968 and 1974, had been a financial disaster. The contract documents did not fully provide for the difficult geologic conditions that were encountered. Some of the contractor's methods were questionable, but the owner, the Colorado Department of Highways, did not have the administrative tools necessary to cope with the serious disputes that arose. The final cost of the job was more than double the original contract price.

Determined to avoid similar difficulties during construction of the second bore, the Colorado Department of Highways established a contract requirement for a review board to make nonbinding recommendations regarding disputes between the contractor and the owner. The contract provisions did not require immediate organization of the board, but the parties elected to do so—a practice which, for good reason, has become accepted industrywide. The contract requirement was far from explicit regarding the operations of the board but these evolved during the early meetings. Similar DRBs were used on electrical and finish-work contracts for the tunnel and later on two other tunnel contracts and two large bridge projects in western Colorado.

Following the successful experience on the Eisenhower Tunnel, the DRB process was used in 1980 on the El Cajon Hydroelectric Project in Honduras, again with outstanding success. Next, the concept was used in Seattle for construction of the Mt. Baker Ridge Highway Tunnel and then for the tunnel approaches. The concept was also used for construction of the Chambers Creek Tunnel in Tacoma, Washington.

To summarize, during the 10-year period from 1975 to 1985, dispute review boards were initiated on five tunnel projects and four other heavy construction projects.

1.2.4.2 1986 to 1994. The late 1980s witnessed a tremendous increase in acceptance of the DRB concept. By 1988, 24 projects were added to the list, with 75 more by 1991 and an additional 250 by 1994. A tabulation of known DRB uses is included in Appendix A. Although the concept was first implemented on a tunnel project, other types of heavy construction work joined the growing list. Recently, many building projects and projects involving process industries have utilized DRBs, a trend that points to applicability and acceptance in all sectors of the construction industry.

1.2.5 Evolution of Partnering

The practice of partnering has gained considerable prominence in recent years, and this manual would not be complete without considering its relationship to the DRB concept.

Project partnering was introduced to the American construction industry in 1989 by the U.S. Army Corps of Engineers. The concept involves building a mutual understanding of goals and objectives among key people on the job, from both the contractor's side and the owner's side. It focuses on their development of and commitment to a partnership charter for the prosecution of the work. Details on how the process functions are available from the Associated General Contractors of America (AGC) and other organizations.

Partnering has been credited with a significant reduction in the incidence of claims in several large organizations such as the U.S. Army Corps of Engineers, the Federal Highway Administration, and some state departments of transportation. The process achieves its most dramatic success when both the contractor and the owner are committed and when a problem resolution hierarchy is established that extends to the upper levels of management.

Some of the most enthusiastic advocates of partnering agree that a dispute review board may still be needed as a safety net or backstop for the settlement of difficult problems. One owner, the Washington State Department of Transportation, uses both partnering and the DRB process on many of its projects.

The positive (as opposed to adversarial) attitudes fostered by partnering are fully compatible with the nonadversarial resolution of disputes facilitated by DRBs. In fact, steps are already being taken to combine the two processes.

1.2.6 International Projects

The DRB concept was introduced to international construction on the El Cajon Hydroelectric Project in Honduras in 1980. Following that there was little international DRB activity until recently. Nevertheless, one project deserves mention at this point.

Construction of the Channel Tunnel between England and France was performed under a design-build contract which included all operating facilities as well as the civil work. The contractual dispute resolution process provided for a panel consisting of a president, two members appointed by each of the two parties, and two alternates similarly appointed. The entire five-member panel heard all disputes, but each decision was made by the president and his selection of one of each of the two members appointed by each of the parties. Any unanimous decision of the three-member panel was binding upon both parties unless and until revised upon appeal to arbitration.

The panel made recommendations on 16 disputes with a total value of $3 billion. Three of these recommendations were not accepted and were appealed to arbitration. The first recommendation was accepted after the arbitration was dropped. The second was partially altered during the arbitration. The third was referred back to the panel for a full decision and eventually settled.

The provisions for this dispute settlement process did not call the panel a dispute review board, and the process did not conform to the criteria developed over the years for the conventional DRB process. One of the principal requirements of a DRB is that its recommendations be advisory and not binding on either party. Even more objectionable in the Channel Tunnel process is the fact that even a binding resolution may be overturned. For these reasons, the Channel Tunnel is not included in the DRB statistics recited in this book. Nevertheless, the Channel Tunnel was an unprecedented project with many unique political and contractual features. It is possible that the conventional DRB process would have been less successful than the process actually used. In any case, the project can be considered a milestone in the acceptance of several elements of the DRB concept in international construction work.

At the present time, dispute review boards are in place on large hydroelectric projects in China and India as well as on the

Lesotho Highlands Water Development Project in Africa. Also, the World Bank has now adopted a policy requiring DRBs on its larger projects. For more information on these applications see Section 1.3.

1.2.7 Experience

The use of DRBs has increased exponentially, as shown in Fig. 1.2. As of January 1988, 7 DRB projects were completed and 16 recommendations for resolution were issued and accepted, with no litigation. By February 1991, 21 DRB projects had been completed and 78 recommendations for resolution were issued and accepted, without litigation.

As of January 1994, 68 DRB projects had been completed and 211 disputes were settled. An additional 98 projects were under construction and 172 more were in the planning stage. Construction projects totaling $19 billion have used or plan to use the DRB process. Appendix A is a compilation of all known uses and intended applications as of January 1994.

The two state transportation departments that pioneered the DRB concept—Colorado and Washington—have continued to

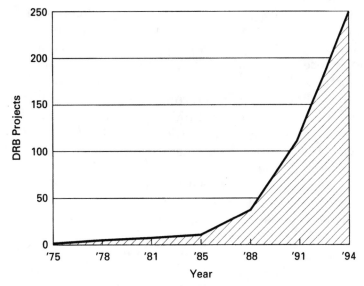

Figure 1.2. Cumulative DRB usage.

use it, thus indicating their satisfaction. To date, Colorado has completed 8 DRB projects; Washington, 20.

Several other agencies undertaking a large number of construction contracts are using the DRB concept quite extensively. They include the following:

1. California Department of Transportation (projects of $7 million and up)
2. Los Angeles Metro (all tunnels and stations for Segment II and following segments)
3. Massachusetts Highway Department (Central Artery and Tunnel projects greater than $10 million)
4. Washington Metropolitan Area Transit Authority
5. Toronto Transit Commission (on surface, underground, and elevated jobs for rapid transit expansion program)
6. San Francisco Bay Area Rapid Transit District (extension program contracts greater than $20 million)
7. State of Maine, Department of Transportation (all five contracts for the Portland Bridge replacement)

The impressive success rate of the DRB concept deserves special examination. Many of the reasons for its success can be found in this book. So far as is known, not one of the over 200 disputes considered by DRBs has gone on through a complete adjudication process. In some cases both parties rejected the recommendation of the DRB, but usually they continued to negotiate and, with the help of the DRB recommendation, were able to resolve the issues. In one case that did proceed to litigation, the court reportedly encouraged the parties to resolve their differences in line with the DRB recommendation. They did so and the dispute was settled.

In the few cases in which the DRB process appeared to fail, good reasons can be found. In one, the model specification provisions for a DRB had been altered, so that if the contractor disagreed with the board's recommendation, a lawsuit had to be filed in order to preserve the active status of the claim. Thus, the opportunity for future negotiation on the basis of the board's recommendation was not available.

In several cases, the DRB was organized after the work was substantially completed and after the parties had adopted somewhat irrevocable, and quite adversarial, positions. Although these cannot be considered true DRB cases, it is notable that even then, when both parties did not accept the DRB recommendation, they usually continued to negotiate and eventually arrived at a settlement.

1.2.8 Construction Industry
Institute Studies and Report

In 1990, the Dispute Prevention and Resolution Task Force of the Construction Industry Institute (CII) embarked on a research project to investigate alternative dispute resolution (ADR) concepts in construction. The effort was headed by M. C. Vorster, Professor of Civil Engineering at Virginia Polytechnic Institute and State University, Blacksburg, Virginia. The project reviewed the full spectrum of ADR techniques, but placed emphasis on dispute review boards "because of their documented success in resolving disputes at the project level." Five specific research objectives were identified:

1. Gain an understanding of the nature of disputes.
2. Study the growing field of ADR techniques in construction.
3. Study the functioning of a dispute review board.
4. Determine whether DRBs are appropriate for the private, commercial, and industrial sectors of the industry.
5. Develop guidelines for implementing DRBs in private, commercial, and industrial construction when appropriate.

The report of the research effort and its findings, made public in July 1993, is the most comprehensive examination of the DRB concept published to date. Of particular importance is its coverage of private construction, a subject which has received limited attention in the past.

In 1992, the Dispute Prevention and Resolution Task Force of CII began a study to assess the effect of various project factors on the frequency of disputes during construction. This study was headed by James Diekmann, Professor of Civil Engineering at the University of Colorado at Boulder.

A predictive model, the disputes potential index, was based on responses from 159 heavy-highway and building and process projects. The model consists of 21 questions which are rated for 17 factors found to be significant in predicting the probability of disputes. A number of factors relate to "people" issues associated with the project's construction. Although the answers to the questions are very subjective, the model seems reliable in evaluating the potential for disputes on these types of projects. The results of the task force's research were presented at the CII annual meeting in August 1994.

The DRB process, by its very nature, helps improve "people" relationships by fostering communication and trust. It also improves the process of communication and dispute resolution.

1.2.9   Outlook for the Future

In recent years, in response to the need for cost-effective alternatives to litigation and arbitration, numerous professional and trade organizations began to study various ADR procedures, and many are endorsing the DRB concept. Some of these organizations are listed below.

Dispute Resolution Organizations

American Arbitration Association

Construction Industry Dispute Avoidance and Resolution Task Force

CPR Institute for Dispute Resolution

Business and Professional Organizations

Construction Industry Institute

Construction Industry Presidents Forum

Associated General Contractors of America

American Underground Association

International Organizations

The World Bank

Institution of Civil Engineers of the United Kingdom

International Committee on Large Dams

International Tunnelling Association

European Bank for Reconstruction and Development

Also, several consulting firms and law firms are offering dispute avoidance and resolution services.

The growing level of interest on the part of private construction and international construction portends increased use of the DRB process in these fields. Considering the successful record of the DRB process, it can be safely predicted that this concept will continue to grow in popularity both in the United States and internationally.

1.3   Essential Elements of the DRB

1.3.1   Introduction

The success of the DRB process can be ascribed to a number of features which are not usually found in other ADR concepts. The following elements are essential to the success of a DRB:

1. All three members of the DRB are neutral and subject to the approval of both parties.

2. All members sign a three-party agreement obligating them to serve both parties equally and fairly.

3. The fees and expenses of the DRB members are shared equally by the parties.

4. The DRB is organized when work begins, before there are any disputes.

5. The DRB keeps abreast of job developments by means of relevant documentation and regular site visits.

6. Either party can refer a dispute to the DRB.

7. An informal but comprehensive hearing is convened promptly.

8. The written recommendations of the DRB are not binding on either party but are admissible as evidence, to the extent permitted by law, in case of later arbitration or litigation.

9. The members are absolved from any personal or professional liability arising from their DRB activities.

Altering or deleting any of these essential elements is a divergence which may place the success of the DRB process at risk.

1.3.2 Overview

The DRB concept can be divided into three principal components:

1. People—impartial, technically proficient, project-knowledge-able, and mutually selected
2. Procedures—simple, straightforward, fair, and efficient, providing for prompt consideration and resolution of disputes
3. Results—(a) encouragement of early dispute resolution (before referral to the board); (b) nonbinding recommendations framed to explain the board's logic and to encourage acceptance by both parties

The following sections address these subjects in greater detail.

1.3.3 Board Member Qualifications

It is essential that both the owner and the contractor have complete confidence in the ability and integrity of each DRB member. The elements that provide this confidence include the board's collective knowledge of and experience with the type of construction involved, interpretation of contract documents, and resolution of contract disputes.

The first two DRB members should be aware of these qualifications and should select the third member for his or her ability (1) to supplement them and (2) to take a leading role in the board's activities.

All three DRB members should be acquainted with the DRB process and be totally committed to its success. To facilitate effective management and administration of the process, it is highly desirable that at least one member of the board have prior DRB experience.

1.3.3.1 Board Member Selection Process. The recommended specification calls for each contracting party to propose a member shortly after contract award. Each nominee must be acceptable to the other party. Once two mutually acceptable members are appointed, they are to confer promptly and nominate a third member, who also must be acceptable to both parties. The parties should make whatever inquiries and evaluations are deemed necessary to ensure that all nominees are acceptable to them. This method of selection promotes the trust that is so essential to the process.

Many public bodies acquire slates of potential board members by advertising in industry publications. The replies are evaluated and selected candidates are interviewed. In other cases, potential candidates are located through inquiries within the industry.

1.3.4 Simple, Straightforward, Fair, and Efficient Procedures

The DRB was conceived (and is most successful) as a method of dispute resolution at the job site. Thus, the procedures should facilitate prompt reference of disputes to the board as soon as job-level negotiations have reached an impasse. Referral to the board only after multiple levels of owner and contractor reviews is inconsistent with the process and counterproductive in terms of time and expense.

Key steps in the procedures include:

1. Prompt organization of DRB

2. Regular DRB meetings and site visits

3. Regular reporting to DRB

4. Prompt referral of disputes to DRB

5. Simple preparation for hearings

6. Informal hearings, with all parties given ample opportunity to present and defend their positions

7. Prompt issuance of written recommendations

The guide specification in Appendix C is based on extensive discussion and consideration by individuals with many years of experience in the implementation of dispute review boards. The guide provides tested and reliable, simple, and straightforward procedures which are known to facilitate smooth and responsive DRB functioning.

1.3.4.1 Keeping the Board Informed Through Meetings and Reports. One of the unique features of the DRB is that it is established to promote resolution of disputes shortly after they arise, while construction is still under way. The board's ability to respond promptly and intelligently requires that it be kept informed of construction activities, progress, and problems.

Each board member should be provided with a complete set of contract documents and be included on the distribution list for periodic progress reports and progress meeting minutes. The board should visit the site on a regular basis so it can observe the progress of the work firsthand, meet with both parties, and discuss problems and proposed solutions.

1.3.4.2 Prompt Referrals to DRB. In keeping with the philosophy of prompt on-site problem resolution, the DRB should be available to either party on fairly short notice after the owner and contractor have reached an impasse in negotiations. Time-consuming reviews off site by upper-tier management are not normally required before the board considers a dispute. Little if any evidence supports the notion that easy access to the DRB process proliferates dispute referrals. Rather, it has been repeatedly found that the presence of the board encourages the participants to resolve their differences and thus avoid disputes. The DRB should encourage the parties to negotiate in good faith and not simply refer all disputes to the board.

1.3.4.3 Preparation for Hearing. Board consideration of a dispute nearly always entails a review of correspondence and related project documents. Rather than each party preparing a compilation of factual information, it is more efficient for the parties to prepare a joint compilation, typically by having the claimant prepare a set of materials and then submit it to the other party for possible supplementation. For various reasons, this is often not done. All documentation, as well as position briefs by each party, should be provided to the board at least one week prior to the hearing.

1.3.4.4 Hearings. DRB hearings are informal and are usually conducted at the job site with the board chair presiding. Each party is given ample time to present its position and rebut that of the other. See Section 2.3 for hearing procedures.

1.3.5 The DRB Recommendation

The board's output is its written recommendation for resolution of the dispute. (A sample recommendation is included in Appendix D.) It tells the parties how three informed, knowledgeable people believe the dispute should be resolved.

Four features are basic to every recommendation. First is a short statement of the substance of the dispute. Next is a reiteration of the positions of both parties. The remaining features are the recommendation and the reasons and the logic that led to the recommendation. Both parties must fully understand why the board recommended as it did. The recommendation should be issued as soon as possible, usually a few weeks after the hearing.

1.3.6 DRB Methodology Checklist

Table 1.1 provides a useful checklist for those considering the DRB process. It lists important issues developed in the CII task force report along with comments from the authors.

1.4 Benefits

Use of a dispute review board provides benefits to all participants in the construction process—and to the project. These benefits accrue in terms of both prevention and resolution of disputes.

1.4.1 Dispute Prevention Benefits

The very existence of a readily available, mutually acceptable dispute resolution process which utilizes a panel of mutually

Table 1.1. DRB Methodology Checklist

Use this checklist to assess compliance of a particular DRB
with the classic methodology developed by ASCE/UTRC.
There should be a positive response to all 22 statements.

CII task force report	Authors' comment
Contract Requirements	
1. The intention to establish a board is noted in the instructions to bidders.	This is thought to indicate an enlightened owner and may encourage lower bids.
2. The provisions for establishing the board are set out in the contract.	This enables both parties to understand their rights and responsibilities with respect to setting up the DRB.
3. The provisions for establishing a board do not preclude either the owner or the contractor from resorting to other methods for final dispute settlement.	The DRB output is neither final nor binding.
Member Qualifications	
4. Members are neutral, able to serve owner and contractor equally with no conflict of interest.	This is critical to the process.
5. Board members have acknowledged technical expertise in the type of work being undertaken.	This promotes (a) confidence that the board members understand the facts, issues, and contract requirements, and (b) efficiency.
6. All parties agree on selection and appointment of all board members.	This is critical to the process.
Member Selection	
7. Owner and contractor each nominate one member. These two members select the third member to act as chair.	This permits each party to pick one neutral, subject to conflict-of-interest requirements and other party's approval.
8. All parties agree on selection and appointment of all board members.	"Hands on" involvement in the process promotes confidence.

Table 1.1. DRB Methodology Checklist (*Continued*)

Use this checklist to assess compliance of a particular DRB with the classic methodology developed by ASCE/UTRC. There should be a positive response to all 22 statements.

CII task force report	Authors' comment
Operating Procedures	
9. Board members receive regular, written progress reports and remain informed of the status of the work.	Not special reports but periodic reports and progress meeting minutes which are part of normal contract administration. Time required for board review is modest.
10. Board meetings are held on the job site at regular intervals, not exceeding 4 months.	This is critical. Resist temptation to cancel meetings because there are no problems. It deprives the DRB of opportunity to build familiarity with project and its participants.
11. Presentations to the board are made by field project managers completely involved in the process.	Firsthand accounts are valuable.
12. Either owner or contractor is able to appeal any decision, action, order, claim, or controversy to the board at any time.	It is presumed that good-faith, bilateral negotiations have been conducted. However, the practice of some owners interposing numerous procedural prerequisites or levels of review before going to the DRB diminishes many of the advantages of the DRB.
13. Both owner and contractor are adequately represented at all hearings; rebuttal and requests for clarification are permitted.	Adequate representation refers to "key players," not counsel. Experience has shown that principals know when they have said enough.
14. Board recommendations are in writing and are made directly to the project participants, who are responsible for accepting, appealing, or rejecting recommendations.	The written recommendation, with rationale, demonstrates the DRB's understanding of the dispute. The rationale/explanation helps persuade the disappointed party to accept the recommendation.

Table 1.1. DRB Methodology Checklist (*Continued*)

Use this checklist to assess compliance of a particular DRB
with the classic methodology developed by ASCE/UTRC.
There should be a positive response to all **22** statements.

CII task force report	Authors' comment
Timing and Sequence of Events	
15. Board selection and appointment are made within 8 weeks of notice to proceed with contract work.	Having the DRB in place early permits it to become acquainted with the project and its participants. Having it in place before disputes are likely to arise prevents posturing or vacillation regarding the process.
16. Appeals are made to the board as soon as possible and the board handles issues current at the time of appeal.	The "real time" component promotes prevention and item-by-item resolution.
17. Written recommendations of the board and the reasoning supporting the recommendations are made available to the project participants within 2 weeks of an appeal.	Two weeks is desirable, but occasionally difficult to achieve. On the other hand, some recommendations can be issued in a matter of hours or days.
Limitations of Authority	
18. Board members do not act as consultants and do not give advice on the conduct of the work.	To do so would obviously compromise neutrality.
19. The board does not usurp either the owner's or the contractor's authority to direct the work as provided in the contract.	The DRB's role is to: (a) review and (b) make recommendations for resolution of disputes presented to it.
Subsequent Proceedings	
20. The recommendations of the board are not binding and may be rejected by either owner or contractor.	This promotes focus on the most relevant evidence and facilitates informal procedures.

Table 1.1. DRB Methodology Checklist (*Continued*)

Use this checklist to assess compliance of a particular DRB
with the classic methodology developed by ASCE/UTRC.
There should be a positive response to all 22 statements.

CII task force report	Authors' comment
Subsequent Proceedings	
21. The written recommendations of the board and the reasoning supporting the recommendations are admissible as evidence in any subsequent dispute resolution procedure.	This promotes focus on the most relevant evidence and facilitates informal procedures.
Cost	
22. The cost of the board is borne equally by the owner and the contractor.	This is consistent with the notion of the DRB being a neutral panel.

SOURCE: As developed by Professor M. C. Vorster, Virginia Polytechnic Institute and State University.

selected and technically knowledgeable neutrals tends to promote bilateral agreement on matters that have historically been referred to third-party adjudication after a long and acrimonious period of posturing. Experience has shown that a DRB facilitates positive relations, open communication, and the trust and cooperation associated with partnering. There are several reasons for this. Participants to the process are effectively deprived of any opportunity to posture—they do not want to lose their credibility with the DRB by taking tenuous or extreme positions. In addition, since the typical DRB handles disputes on an individual basis, the aggregation of claims is minimized and there is generally not an ever-growing backlog of unresolved claims creating an atmosphere that fosters acrimony.

On DRB projects the parties are encouraged to identify, evaluate, and deal with claims and disputes in a prompt, businesslike manner. At each regular meeting the DRB asks about any potential disputes and also requests a status report on claims that may be on a future agenda. In this manner, the parties focus on early identification and analysis, and prompt resolution, while remaining aware of the board's availability in the event of an impasse.

1.4.2 Dispute Resolution Benefits

A principal benefit of a DRB is its very high resolution rate—almost 100 percent. It is more successful than any other method of alternative dispute resolution for construction disputes. Several unique factors account for this statistic. A DRB provides the parties with an impartial forum and an informed and rational basis for resolution of their dispute. The members of a typical board have knowledge and experience with (1) the design and construction issues germane to the project, (2) the interpretation and application of contract documents, (3) the process of dispute resolution, and (4) the specific design and construction for the project. Since both parties have agreed to the board members *and* the process in advance of any dispute, the parties are normally favorably predisposed to DRB proceedings.

A second tangible benefit is the relative cost effectiveness of the DRB method compared with other ADR methods and with litigation. As a "standing neutral" methodology, the DRB process typically addresses disputes very soon after impasse in bilateral negotiations. This greatly reduces transaction costs, such as legal and consultant fees, as well as lost productive time of key participants for the contracting parties. Early resolution also accords the benefit of a better-informed decision, because eyewitnesses are readily available and, in many instances, the board can actually observe the field condition or construction operation that is the basis for a claim.

Cost savings actually begin with lower bids because of a reduced bid risk premium. It is well established that fair contracting practices in general result in lower bids, for they reduce contingencies and convey an enlightened and positive owner attitude to all bidders. When the owner's bidding documents indicate that a DRB will be used to resolve disputes, prospective contractors are advised that if disputes do occur, they will be dealt with expeditiously by a mutually selected panel of technically knowledgeable neutrals. Thus, the risks of long delays in resolving disputes and of substantial out-of-pocket transaction costs are reduced or eliminated. Further, earlier resolution means an earlier start to the payment process for DRB contract modification recommendations accepted by the owner.

1.5 Perceived Barriers

1.5.1 Introduction

Owners first considering the use of DRBs may justifiably identify issues that they perceive to be of concern. Opponents of the process have also advanced arguments against DRBs. This section identifies and addresses those concerns.

1.5.2 The Perception That a DRB Is a Departure from Traditional Roles and Practices

It is true that the DRB process is comparatively new. So are most methods of alternative dispute resolution. What needs to be understood, however, is that DRBs evolved to meet a demonstrated need: prompt, informal, neutral, nonbinding dispute resolution at the job-site level. DRBs have convincingly demonstrated the satisfaction of that need. With successful use on hundreds of construction projects worth billions of dollars in several countries, DRBs are no longer experimental.

In reality, a DRB provides a job-site dispute resolution device similar to the historic practice of the design professional or owner's project manager being perceived as a neutral decision maker by both parties to the contract (the "architect" in early AIA contracts and the "engineer" in FIDIC contracts). Today it is widely recognized that, in practice, the contractor has considerable difficulty in accepting a design professional or project manager compensated by the owner as a true neutral. Perhaps as a result, the recently published U.K. Institution of Civil Engineers' *New Engineering Contract* provides for a mutually selected neutral "adjudicator."

A DRB does not supplant the decision-making responsibility or authority of the owner, the engineer, the construction manager, or the contractor. It can actually facilitate such decision making. A clear statement of the claim by the contractor and a responsible evaluation by the owner or engineer or construction manager are required in any scenario. The typical DRB timetable forces such steps to be taken promptly. And, once they are completed, the parties may find there is enough common ground to get to closure. In addition, the engineer or construction manager is not faced with a difficult conflict of interest: on the one hand, being the owner's designer/adviser/consultant; and on the other hand, being the presumed or titular neutral decider of disputes.

Significantly, the third-party advisory recommendation of a DRB provides justification for public owners, who sometimes are understandably sensitive to the potential for taxpayer and media attention associated with recommendations that additional compensation be paid to a contractor.

In the end, any dispute that the parties cannot resolve will be referred to a neutral forum—be it DRB, arbitration, or litigation. Experience and common sense make it clear that the sooner the forum is utilized, the lower the cost. And if that forum has design and construction experience and project-specific knowledge, the quality of its output will be superior.

1.5.3 The Perception That DRBs Do Not Add Value

Limited owner budgets for construction projects are a given. However, the fundamental cost-effectiveness calculus of DRBs readily demonstrates that establishing and operating a DRB is a highly leveraged investment, even if there are no disputes. Although it is difficult to quantify the benefits in dollars, as discussed above, it has been amply demonstrated that such benefits exist. Consider the following:

1. Lower bids
2. Better communication and less acrimony on the job site
3. Timely and cost-effective resolution of issues at the job-site level
4. Fewer claims
5. Reduced transaction costs

1.5.4 The Perception That a DRB Will Impose Its Own Concepts of Fairness and Equity

As we have seen, a DRB is a key component in an overall program of modern contracting practices and rational risk allocation. Nonetheless, an owner who does not subscribe to all components of such a program can still utilize a DRB successfully. That is, any owner who is committed to the timely, fair, and cost-effective resolution of disputes can benefit from a DRB. A competent and conscientious board will not impose its own ideas of fairness and equity on the parties. Rather, it will strive for a recommendation consistent with the contract language which forms the basis of the parties' agreement. Indeed, the standard three-party agreement requires a DRB to comply with applicable laws and contract provisions. As a further safeguard, the owner has the option of rejecting any recommendation with which it disagrees.

1.5.5 The Perception That the Low-Threshold Effort Promotes Claims

Users might initially believe that since the effort and expense of submitting a dispute to a DRB are relatively small, a contractor might utilize the process extensively to test the viability of seemingly marginal claims. This practice has not been borne out by experience. To the contrary, it has been observed that contractors do not want to face the loss of credibility that would likely result from asking a board to consider a nonmeritorious claim. Statistical evidence shows that numerous projects with DRBs have had *no* disputes.

1.5.6 The Perception That a Given Board Is Unqualified or Biased

The many satisfied users of DRBs have not experienced much difficulty in obtaining members with the qualifications deemed appropriate for their projects. There is little excuse for an unqualified board when the contracting parties are expected to apply appropriate selection criteria. (Some public owners solicit board members through an advertised request for qualifications (RFQ), a process that often culminates in personal interviews and evaluation against established criteria, such as construction and dispute resolution experience.) Given the standard provision that member qualifications are subject to review and approval by both contracting parties, there is really no valid basis for alleging that the parties will end up with an unqualified board.

Without question, in addition to technical competence, each board member must have a neutrality or objectivity that is above reproach. This neutrality is a key to the success of DRBs. The conflict-of-interest standards in the guide specification, coupled with the ability of either contracting party to veto a nominee, put the ability to select true neutrals within the power of the contracting parties.

1.5.7 The Perception That a Given Board Will Not Be Well Informed

A board with the requisite experience, neutrality, and integrity will by definition be conscientious as well. And a conscientious DRB will strive to be well informed. As a practical matter, the only way a board will be uninformed is if the contracting parties abdicate their responsibilities. For example, standard practice is that plans and specifications are forwarded to the board as soon as it is formally established. In addition, copies of regularly produced progress reports and meeting minutes should be submitted to board members so that they are kept abreast of activities on the site. Finally, the board is charged with making periodic visits to the site, even when no disputes are to be heard. The failure to implement these practices by making a relatively modest investment in board member fees and expenses will have an adverse effect on the DRB's ability to become familiar with the project and its key participants. This "learning curve" effort is essential to the board's effectiveness.

1.5.8 The Argument That a DRB Will Prolong the Claims Process

Some have asserted that a DRB adds another step to a project's claims-and-disputes process. While true in absolute terms, the DRB is almost always the last step. The adage "Justice delayed is justice denied" has some application to the DRB process. In keeping with the philosophy that the DRB was originally conceived (and works best) as a method of job-site dispute resolution, the guide specification contemplates prompt board action. Sometimes complex disputes or unavoidable schedule conflicts of DRB members may justify a modest delay. As long as an effort is made to hold hearings promptly after they are requested, and to issue recommendations promptly after the hearings are completed, there should not be any delays. Though this can sometimes place a substantial burden on board members, it is critical to the process. If the contracting parties and the DRB are committed to timeliness, delays should not be a problem.

1.5.9 The Argument That Disclosure of Supporting Documentation Will Be Prejudicial

Typical DRB procedure involves the prehearing submission of short narrative statements of position from the contracting parties, usually accompanied or preceded by supporting documentation. Some might object that this documentation provides the parties with "free discovery." However, as a practical matter, supporting documentation is likely to surface early in any event, so this is not a valid criticism.

1.5.10 The Argument That DRB Procedures Introduce Acrimony or Promote Posturing

Properly conducted, the DRB process prevents or reduces acrimony. Rather than fostering a "win-lose" dichotomy, the process often results in a "win-win" situation. Mutual cooperation eliminates transaction expenses (e.g., legal and expert fees), which are normally "sunk" costs to both parties. In addition, the periodic board meetings bring key participants face to face to rationally address their respective positions.

1.5.11 The Argument That DRBs Lack Legal Procedures and Standards

Some commentators have opined that the DRB's relatively informal fact-finding procedure, characterized by limited documentary discovery and unsworn "testimony" (without cross-examination) elicited by nonlawyers, is a drawback. The concerns relate to veracity and relevance, among other things. To a great extent, these objections miss the mark, since true disputes of material fact seldom remain after the hearing process. The extensive documentation in most projects, as well as the ready availability of knowledgeable witnesses, minimizes factual disputes.

1.6 Variations

For the purposes of this section, ASCE DRBs are defined as those which basically follow the principles set forth in the predecessor documents published by the ASCE in 1989, *Avoiding and Resolving Disputes in Underground Construction,* and in 1991, *Avoiding and Resolving Disputes During Construction.* Non-ASCE DRBs are those which depart from the principles and specifications in those ASCE booklets.

1.6.1 ASCE DRBs

Several variations in the organization and functioning of a DRB have been used, and other variations have been proposed. These are outlined below, together with some of the advantages and disadvantages of each. Some of the variations have been used with success, and some others offer possibilities for success when used in certain circumstances. Others have proved to be substantially flawed. Some of these variations are mentioned elsewhere in this manual but are included here for completeness.

1.6.2 Structural Variations

1.6.2.1 One-Person DRB. The DRB process can operate with only one member and has done so successfully on several occasions. For most projects, it is preferable to have the benefit of three separate viewpoints. A one-person DRB is acceptable when both parties are comfortable with only one member and when the project is too small to warrant a three-member DRB.

1.6.2.2 Interlocking DRB Member. When a number of separate contracts are related as parts of a larger system, there are advantages to having a single DRB member serve on more than one board. The interlocking member provides consistency in the solution of problems among the contracts.

1.6.2.3 Five-Person DRB. The five-member DRB, applicable to large, complex projects involving many construction disciplines, was used on construction of the Channel Tunnel between England and France.

Two members are nominated by each party and a chairperson is selected by both. All members receive regular reports and attend the scheduled meetings and all dispute hearings. The chairperson selects two of the four other members to form a three-member panel for each dispute hearing. The advantage is the ability to choose among four members in shaping a hearing panel according to particular fields of expertise. The disadvantage is the increased cost of additional members, so this option is attractive only for projects with many technical disciplines.

1.6.2.4 Multiple-Contract DRB. When an owner is performing two or more construction contracts with a physical interface in the same general geographic area, efficiencies can be achieved by using a single DRB. Members can be selected through a third party or by having all the contractors agree on the candidates. This technique has distinct advantages when members of the DRB must travel great distances. It can also be advantageous when there are critical interfaces among separate contractors. The approach can be disadvantageous when separate contracts involve a wide diversity of technologies.

1.6.3 Procedural Variations

1.6.3.1 Standby DRB. On some projects, a DRB is selected promptly but is put on standby until called upon to consider a dispute. This expedient sacrifices the tremendous advantages offered by periodic job-site visits, which not only ensure that DRB members are familiar with the project but also encourage the parties to avoid disputes or to resolve them amicably. Standby DRBs are not recommended.

1.6.3.2 Optional DRB. An owner might be reluctant to specify a DRB, fearing that the successful bidder will not want one. Providing the option of a board makes the DRB process still available if the contractor so desires. This expedient is acceptable only if the option must be exercised immediately upon contract award. Otherwise, it is meaningless.

1.6.3.3 DRB Organized After Dispute Arises. If the initial specification did not provide for a DRB, the owner and the contractor can implement a DRB by executing a change order to the original contract.

1.6.3.4 DRB Involvement with Subcontractor Disputes. In rare cases, the DRB has been informally involved with subcontractors. When handled discreetly, this approach can be beneficial to a project and merits further study. Appropriate test cases would be worthwhile.

1.6.4 Non-ASCE DRBs

1.6.4.1 DRB Recommendations Binding. Binding recommendations should be employed only in special circumstances. One of the reasons for the wide acceptance of the DRB is that its recommendations are not binding. Since this feature has been so successful, it is a mistake to change it without a good reason.

1.6.4.2 Owner–Employee DRBs. An owner may "augment" its dispute resolution procedure with a board composed of its own employees. This ploy is so obvious that it does not deserve further comment.

1.6.4.3 DRB Organized After the Project Is Complete. A DRB organized at the end of the project to handle accumulated disputes is nothing but an informal, nonbinding arbitration panel and should not be called a dispute review board. At this point, the two parties have developed an adversarial relationship and taken "hard" positions. Virtually all the unique advantages of the DRB concept are lost.

1.6.4.4 AAA Dispute Review Board Procedures. In 1993, the National Construction Dispute Resolution Committee (NCDRC) of the American Arbitration Association (AAA), a multidisciplinary group composed of representatives of owners, design professionals, contractors, and subcontractor trade associations, promulgated the American Arbitration Association's Construction Industry Disputes Review Board Procedures.

The AAA procedure outlines a more abbreviated process than the ASCE specification; it is incorporated by reference into the contract rather than being set out in full in the contract test. A key difference is in the process for selecting DRB members. If the parties have not already chosen the three DRB members, the AAA will assist in the selection. The AAA is further available as an administrative resource to assist the parties and the DRB members, if called on, to facilitate the DRB process and to fill vacancies on the DRB.

1.7 Perspectives

1.7.1 Owner's Perspective

The owner normally makes the decision to utilize a DRB. Considerations for the owner are outlined below.

1.7.1.1 Avoiding Conflicting Role of Owner's Representative. In many construction contracts, the owner's authorized representative (engineer, architect, or construction manager) is placed in an awkward position. That individual is required both to articulate the owner's side of the dispute and to make a final ruling on the contractor's claim. Usually the only appeal is to a formal board of contract appeals or to the courts. As a result, the stance of the owner's representative may become relatively rigid, inhibiting the individual's ability to compromise lest he or she be judged derelict in upholding the owner's interests.

The DRB process relieves the owner's representative of the duty to act as "appeals judge" as well as owner's advocate. The typical result is a much less hostile climate for negotiating claims *before* they are escalated to the status of disputes. For the process to work, the owner must (1) specifically relieve the representative of the burden of making final rulings on contractor's claims and (2) require that all disputes that cannot be resolved on the job be submitted to the dispute resolution board.

1.7.1.2 Encouraging Lower Bid Prices. Contractors have been damaged by one-sided, unfair, and unreasonable contracts and by arbitrary and capricious contract administration. Their first defense to the recurrence of adverse consequences is to price their bids selectively, increasing their prices as the owner's reputation for fair play diminishes. Their second defense is to pursue expensive and uncertain litigation after their fears have been realized. These defensive techniques are often applied to unfamiliar or unproved owners.

An owner can mitigate these unwanted actions and signal its intention to deal fairly and cooperatively with the contractor by providing for a DRB in the contract documents. Providing a DRB can temper any possible unfair treatment and, even more significantly, indicate a positive attitude on the part of the owner.

Contractors with completed DRB projects have stated that bid prices were reduced because DRB provisions were included in the contracts. In retrospect, they agree that the reduction was justified.

1.7.1.3 DRBs Do Not Supplant Existing Procedures. Use of a board is not precluded by existing contract provisions. Adding the DRB process generally introduces neutrality much earlier into the dispute resolution procedure. It need not replace any part of the usually specified dispute resolution process. However, existing contract documents should be reviewed and amended to ensure that specified dispute resolution procedures do not conflict with this additional step.

DRB specifications similar to the guide in Appendix C have been used on many projects and can be easily integrated with existing general conditions. One of the most important points for the owner to realize is that the mere existence of the DRB, making regular visits to the site, can be highly beneficial. No restriction should be placed on the board's ability to exercise judgment in accordance with its own background and experience in the construction process.

Owners who have heretofore depended upon the courts to insulate them from taxpayer and media criticism flowing from the negotiation of contractor claims can now, by means of the DRB concept, enjoy the same degree of protection without the exorbitant costs.

1.7.1.4 Owner Observation and Experience. Owners who are not familiar with a DRB may question its usefulness. Attending a DRB meeting can help them gain an appreciation of the process. For example, observing a Seattle Bus Tunnel DRB meeting helped convince the Alaska Power Authority to use a DRB on the Bradley Lake Power Tunnel and Dam contract. Appendix A lists many owners with DRB experience who presumably have formed certain conclusions and opinions as to the efficacy of the process.

1.7.2 Contractor's Perspective

1.7.2.1 Reflection of Owner's Attitude. Providing a DRB indicates the owner's desire to be open-minded and reasonable in solving problems and to pay valid claims promptly during the course of the work rather than litigate long after construction is complete. The best path to the resolution of disputes is undoubtedly through prompt negotiation between the parties themselves. When this approach is not successful, the facts should be presented as soon as possible to an informed and knowledgeable third-party panel for a recommended solution. The final decision is still within control of the parties. This, in essence, is the DRB process.

1.7.2.2 Avoidance of Disputes. The major objective of DRBs is to avoid disputes or resolve them quickly. Unresolved disputes often persist and escalate throughout construction, causing tempers to flare and the work to suffer.

Early resolution is expedited when the involved personnel are readily available and the facts have not been distorted by the passage of time. The dispute should be referred to the board as soon as the parties sense that a satisfactory solution is unlikely.

1.7.3 Attorney's Perspective

1.7.3.1 Nonbinding Nature. Attorneys have questioned the value of a nonbinding recommendation. However, the acceptance rate of DRB recommendations speaks for itself. The process gives both parties an opportunity to be heard by a knowledgeable and trusted panel which has developed an informed opinion. It is difficult for either party to reject a rationally based recommendation in good faith. The mere presence of the DRB has a preventive effect, inspiring the parties to avoid disputes or to settle them without DRB intervention.

1.7.3.2 Admissibility. There is also the question of whether a board's recommendation should be admissible in evidence in a subsequent arbitration or trial. Some attorneys strongly believe that the effectiveness of the DRB is maximized—and the parties have the greatest incentive to adopt the board's recommendation—when they know in advance that the recommendation and rationale will be received in evidence in the event that the dispute is not resolved amicably. Others argue further that inasmuch as the board's findings of fact are based on firsthand observations and relatively recent events, the findings are likely to be accurate and therefore should be available for consideration by the court, a jury, or arbitrators.

There are several valid arguments against admissibility. First of all, what is a DRB recommendation? An expert's report? If so, have the experts been cross-examined on its content? Does it include hearsay? If so, can the recommendation be admitted as evidence under one of the hearsay rule's exceptions? More pragmatically, is it an output of a dispute settlement process, and perhaps nonadmissible? If the parties know that it will be admissible, will they feel compelled to "build the record" and increase the role of their counsel, thereby adding to the time, expense, and formality of the proceeding and at the same time reducing candor and cooperation?

1.7.3.3 Compromises in Traditional Fact Finding. The contemporaneous, "real time" feature of the DRB approach, which distinguishes it from other ADR methods, generally facilitates access to individuals with firsthand knowledge and tends to enhance the accuracy of any findings of fact.

Traditional legal discovery—a time-consuming, expensive process—is not required when disputes are promptly heard. Like mediators and minitrial panelists, board members actively participate in questioning the parties. Their participation can be an effective fact-finding tool, though admittedly not a vigorous cross-examination under oath. Nevertheless, board members have often demonstrated an ability to ask questions essential to determining the operative facts.

1.7.3.4 Expediency. The amount of information presented to a dispute review board in a typical hearing of only a few days would take weeks or months to present at trial. The expertise of the board members expedites the presentation and understanding of factual and technical information. Prior knowledge of the project provides factual background without consuming hearing time. This compressed presentation time is consistent with other successful ADR methods, such as minitrials and mediation.

1.7.3.5 Other Considerations. With DRBs, attorneys are still involved in the construction process. However, their time and effort are directed toward problem solving and dispute resolution rather than litigation. In the unlikely event that the dispute is not resolved by the DRB recommendation, counsel will be prepared to litigate the case sooner, and at lower cost. With a clearer understanding of facts and issues, the attorneys will be able to agree on many facts, reduce discovery costs, and proceed with less hostility between the parties.

In practice, attorneys seldom attend DRB hearings, although they are not usually barred from attending. For disputes that involve major points of law, attorneys do occasionally attend. There is some concern that attorneys as advocates (as opposed to advisers) tend to make the process adversarial and unnecessarily formal. The entire thrust of the DRB process is to promote cooperation and minimize adversity in dispute resolution.

1.7.4 Dispute Review Board Member Perspective

1.7.4.1 Neutrality and Effectiveness. The success of the DRB process is highly dependent on the integrity, knowledge, and experience of the members.

All board members as well as all owner and contractor personnel need to understand that individual DRB members are not the "representative" or "advocate" of the party which selected them. The entire board must function and always appear as an objective, impartial, and independent body.

If the DRB ever believes that the process could work better with other board members, it should offer to step aside. This necessity would arise if the board senses that either the owner or contractor has lost trust in its impartiality or judgment. The same admonition applies to individual members.

1.7.4.2 Board Members Are Not Consultants. The board and its members are specifically forbidden to give consulting advice to either party. The reason is obvious. The DRB's position would be compromised if such advice should later be drawn into a contract dispute. On the other hand, the board cannot be completely passive. During its regular site visits, it will ask questions and seek explanations in order to fully understand the technicalities of the work and to keep abreast of developments. The parties will get certain messages from these exchanges, and care must be taken to avoid misunderstandings.

1.7.4.3 Initiative. The board should be as proactive as the occasion demands. Sometimes the parties must be urged to disclose potential claims and bring problems into the open. Sometimes the parties procrastinate in reviewing each other's documentation or in conducting negotiations. The board should be innovative in devising methods to break such logjams. One possibility is to schedule a hearing on the dispute for some future date. If, before that date, the parties can demonstrate that they are making progress, the hearing can be canceled. The parties might even resolve the dispute before the hearing date arrives!

The board is endowed with considerable power and it should not hesitate to use that power when necessary. If one party attempts to delay or curtail the board's legitimate activities, the board should take whatever action it deems to be appropriate. Its responsibility to the parties demands this.

If, at any time, it becomes apparent that either party has lost faith in a member of the board, that member should step aside. Regardless of the merits of the occasion, the credibility of the DRB concept should never be sacrificed to individual feelings.

2
Practice

2.0 Member Selection

2.0.1 Introduction

Selection of DRB members is critical to the entire DRB process. The criteria for board membership and the procedures for organizing the DRB are given in detail in the guide specification in Appendix C. This chapter describes how the process works and points out potential problems to be avoided.

2.0.2 General

2.0.2.1 Prompt Establishment. A recurring concern is procrastination by one or both parties in the selection and approval of the first two board members. While occupied with the countless details which must be attended to in getting the work started, the parties may overlook the importance of organizing the DRB quickly so it will be there when the work begins. Yet disputes are often generated by events which occur in the early stages of the work. If the board is not on hand when these events happen, it will be unable to respond in a timely manner.

2.0.2.2 Complete Confidence and Satisfaction. One of the essential elements in the DRB process is that each party be completely satisfied with every board member. If a party is not comfortable with a nomination, it has the right to disapprove, and the appointing party should honor this right. Each party should make clear that it will not take offense if the other party rejects a nomination and will honor that commitment should the situation arise.

The recommended three-party agreement allows the nominating party to terminate a board member when necessary. Although this situation rarely arises, the essence of the DRB process requires that all parties have the utmost confidence in the DRB and its members. The DRB should, by its actions and conduct, maintain that respect. If for any reason that confidence is lost, both parties and the DRB should cooperate in taking corrective action.

2.0.2.3 Variations. In some DRB cases, the guide specification has been changed so that each party nominates three prospective DRB members. Each party then selects one member from the other's list. This process has been used successfully with a number of ADR methods. Although the practice has been criticized by some, it appears to expedite the organization of the DRB. So long as the process observes all the qualifications and approval criteria and satisfies both parties, it should be acceptable.

2.0.3 Avoiding Even the Appearance of Partiality

In order to reinforce the requirement to avoid even the perception of partiality among DRB members, paragraph 1.02.B.2(c) of the guide specification severely limits the appointment of former employees of either party. In the past, when this requirement was much more lenient, individual specifications relaxed it even more. Some owners were even known to adopt a policy of appointing only retired former employees.

In many cases, the former employee may in fact be completely impartial and never allow past relationships to affect his or her judgment. However, the obvious perception that this person might be biased can lead to dissatisfaction with the board and the entire DRB process. If the board issues a recommendation which appears to favor one party, even with complete justification, there will always remain the question of whether the former employee exerted undue influence over the other members. There may even be times when the former employee, in order to avoid criticism by other members, deliberately leans in the other direction. Although this action may appear commendable, it still dilutes the complete objectivity and impartiality of the board. Even if the specification allows, it is recommended that, except in particularly unusual circumstances, the nomination of a former employee be avoided.

Another question concerns the appointment to the board of a full-time employee of a contractor, a consulting firm, or a design firm. Even though the member's employer may generate no conflict of interest at the time, events later on may alter that situation. Since many full-time employees are certainly qualified as potential DRB members, it is not considered prudent to arbitrarily bar them from serving on a DRB. Therefore, whenever this issue arises, the parties should objectively consider all the relevant factors present in the situation and act accordingly. Each party must remember that both sides must be entirely comfortable with all members of the board.

Another potential concern arises when a certain person is consistently nominated by contractors, and another certain party is consistently nominated by owners. A corollary is when a certain contractor or a certain owner consistently nominates some other specific person. Sooner or later, a perception of partiality develops and the credibility of the entire DRB process may be weakened.

It would be difficult to draft a specification which addresses all possibilities of perceived partiality. However, the parties have complete control of this situation and they should be aware of the possible consequences of an indiscreet nomination. Each party should remember that the other party is entitled to feel comfortable with a nomination. Neither party should refrain from making what it feels is a valid objection to a nomination simply out of fear of offending the other party. By the same token, neither party should take offense at the other's valid rejection.

2.0.4 Qualifications and Selection of First Two Members

The model specification describes the desirable attributes of a DRB member. These can be elaborated upon as follows:

1. Complete neutrality and impartiality
2. Freedom from conflict of interest

3. Experience with type of construction involved

4. Knowledge of construction methods to be used

5. Experience with interpretation of contract documents

6. Experience with resolution of construction disputes

7. Knowledge of the DRB process

8. Dedication to the objective of the DRB process

Frequently, both the contractor and the owner will be acquainted with or have knowledge of one or more candidates having these qualifications. The selection is then based upon this knowledge. If a party does not have such knowledge, it can obtain leads from someone who has had DRB experience.

Many owners, particularly those who plan to have a number of DRBs, may prefer to use a more formal method of selection. Usually they advertise in trade publications and obtain qualification data from a number of candidates. The responses are evaluated, a few individuals are interviewed, and a selection is made. Figure 2.1 summarizes the board member selection process. See Appendix C for details.

---

1. Identify experience desired.

2. Identify candidates with desired experience.

3. Evaluate overall qualifications of potential candidates.

4. Interview selected candidates.

5. Select candidates.

6. Negotiate compensation.

7. Receive disclosure statement from selected candidate.
   - Résumé of experience
   - Previous involvement with project
   - Relationships with all parties involved in the construction
   - Relationships with key members of all parties

8. Nominate candidate.

9. Receive approval of other party.

Figure 2.1. Board member selection process.

With the rapidly growing use of the DRB concept, some have expressed concern that an adequate supply of qualified potential members will become exhausted. Although there is little evidence of such a trend, it does appear wise to give consideration to the appointment of untried but otherwise qualified candidates to new DRBs. This not only will help ensure an adequate pool of qualified candidates; it will also serve to nullify any notion that some DRB members are forming an "old boys' club."

2.0.5 Selecting the Third Member

Subject to the approval of both parties, the first two members are responsible for the selection of the third. If these two are already acquainted, a telephone conference may be all that is needed. In some cases, it is necessary to circulate the résumé of a proposed third member. In other cases, it may be advisable for the first two members to meet personally and discuss possible candidates. In addition to reviewing a potential third member's résumé, the first two members may wish to interview the candidate, jointly and in person.

The selection of the third member is very important. In addition to possessing the standard qualifications, the third member should be able to supplement the experience and background of the first two members. The third member is often selected to chair the board. However, this is not required. The chair should be appointed for his or her ability to take charge and lead the DRB activities to a successful conclusion.

2.0.6 Lawyers on a DRB

There has been some controversy as to whether a lawyer should be appointed to a DRB. Many lawyers meet the requirements outlined in the model specification. Some hold degrees in engineering and have practiced law involving construction cases. In fact, several DRBs have included lawyers as members, all with commendable results.

A number of lawyers have demonstrated a keen interest in resolving disputes without recourse to litigation and are strongly supportive of the DRB concept. So long as a lawyer is dedicated to the DRB process and meets the other criteria for membership, there is no reason that he or she should not be eligible for appointment.

The participation of lawyers in other phases of the DRB process is addressed in Sections 1.7.3 and 2.3.2.

2.0.7 Three-Party Agreement

The three-party agreement is the contract that binds the DRB members and the contracting parties. It establishes the scope of the work, the responsibilities of the parties, the duration of the agreement, the manner of payment, and legal relations. It is usually executed at the first DRB meeting. A suggested three-party agreement similar to that used on many projects is found in Appendix C.

2.1 Operation of the Board

2.1.1 Organization

Immediately after selection and approval of the three members, the board and the parties establish a date for the first DRB meeting. The board members usually meet privately beforehand to become acquainted and to address the following matters:

1. Select a chairperson, if one is not already established.

2. Brief inexperienced DRB members on the process. Brief one another on project background.

3. Discuss and affirm the principle that each board member is to be impartial and neutral in all actions. Discuss standards of conduct. Once the board is constituted, each member's connection to the nominating party should promptly disappear.

4. Discuss and affirm the principle that all project-related communications between the DRB and the contracting parties be made through the board chairperson, except during meetings with the parties and via distribution of documents to all three members.

5. Discuss operating procedures. These will also be reviewed with the parties at the first meeting. Typical procedures to be discussed include:
   - The time and level of effort expected for review of progress reports and other materials
   - Standard agenda for regular meetings
   - Minutes—responsibility, extent, format
   - Scheduling future meetings
   - Periodic reports desired—progress reports, progress meeting minutes, change orders, schedule updates, and so forth
   - Travel arrangements for regular meetings, including mode of travel, arrival and departure times, hotel reservations, and rental car arrangements
   - Meeting room arrangement and seating at board meetings
   - Luncheon arrangements
   - Billings—when, to whom, form of invoice, and approvals

2.1.2 First Meeting

At the first meeting with the parties, the board members present the DRB's actions noted above, encourage discussion, solicit suggestions for additions and revisions, and request concurrence. The board chairperson may confirm this in writing to all parties. A list of names, mail and E-mail addresses, and phone and fax numbers of all parties should be compiled.

Discussion at the first meeting should include:

1. The role of the DRB as a proactive board. The board does not usurp the discretion, authority, or decision-making power of either party. Rather, when required, it takes positive steps to encourage settlement of disputes without formal referral to the board. If it becomes clear that the parties cannot resolve their differences, the DRB encourages prompt referral to the board. It manages the dispute review process in a businesslike fashion and responds promptly to the needs of the parties for its legitimate services.

2. The contractual procedure for bringing disputes before the board. This procedure must be thoroughly understood by both parties. Additional clarification is often required prior to the actual referral of a dispute.

3. How dispute documentation should be presented to the board. Details are elaborated on for a specific dispute.

4. The specific documents required by the board. These often include a copy of the contract and bid abstract, a summary of the contractor's basic methods of construction, and the contractor's approved schedule. The basic contract documents should have already been distributed to the board members.

5. The principle that all project-related communications between the board members and the parties be made via the chairperson, except during meetings with the parties. The parties shall not contact any member of the board other than the chairperson. All written correspondence between one party and the chairperson is copied to the other party and the other DRB members.

6. The rule that restricts the board from giving consulting advice to either party. During meetings, DRB members will refrain from expressing opinions on the merits of disputes or potential disputes.

7. The fact that operating procedures are flexible and should be changed as required and agreed to by all parties.

2.1.3 Regular Meetings

Meetings are normally scheduled every 3 months. Frequency of regular meetings is set with the understanding that the schedule is flexible and may change as the work progresses—depending on the work in progress, the number of problems that arise, and the desires of the parties. It is deemed "penny wise and pound foolish" to avoid the cost of these meetings, since important benefits are lost.

Without actually giving consulting advice, the DRB can often comment on the merits of various courses of action. The board must, of course, be extremely careful that it does not compromise its role or dilute its relationship with either party.

2.1.3.1 Format for Regular Meeting. All parties should agree to the general format of the meeting agenda. The owner (or its architect, engineer, or construction manager), with input from the contractor, often prepares and distributes the agenda. This responsibility may also be assigned to the DRB chairperson. The agenda can vary as befits the project and the circumstances, and will generally include as a minimum the following items:

1. The board chairperson convenes the DRB meeting and requests approval of the minutes of the previous meeting.
2. The contractor describes the work accomplished since the last meeting, the status of the work schedule, plans for future work, potential claims, disputes and other controversies, and proposed solutions.
3. The owner (or its architect, engineer, or construction manager) describes the work schedule, potential problems or disputes, and other controversies.
4. The status of past problems and disputes is summarized.
5. Field observation is scheduled for all active segments of the work. Board members are accompanied by both contractor and owner personnel.

Draft minutes of each meeting should be prepared by the owner and distributed to all parties for approval. After finalization, they are again distributed. In some cases, the DRB chairperson prepares the minutes.

2.1.4 Special Meetings

Special meetings may be called as necessary to hear a dispute or to consider some emergency, unforeseen condition, or other matter demanding prompt board observation, attention, or consideration.

2.2 Referral of a Dispute to the Board

2.2.1 Early Referral

For maximum effectiveness, the board should become involved as soon as it becomes clear that a bona fide dispute exists. Disputes should be taken to the board as soon as either party believes that a negotiated settlement is unlikely.

The primary objective of the DRB process is to facilitate the early resolution of disputes by informal, nonadversarial means. The guide specification promotes that objective. Needless conflict arises when restrictive procedural steps set forth in other provisions of the contract conflict with the DRB provisions covering referral of disputes to the board. Care should be taken to eliminate all such impediments from the contract documents.

Some owners have included procedural requirements in other sections of the contract calling for the contractor to submit a fully documented and quantified claim to the owner, have the claim denied, and exhaust all remedies provided by the contract short of litigation or arbitration before referral of a dispute to the DRB. Such contractual language prevents the DRB from becoming involved in a case until long after the genesis of the dispute. In some instances, procedural objection on the part of the owner has resulted in the DRB conducting hearings and making recommendations solely on the issue of whether the dispute could be submitted to the DRB under the terms of the contract. Contractual provisions requiring these procedures are needlessly time-consuming and negate the very concept of rapid, equitable resolution of disputes through the DRB process.

2.2.2 Limitations

Contract specifications should provide that either the contractor or the owner may submit any issue to the DRB once it becomes clear, in the opinion of either party, that a dispute exists and is not likely to be resolved without DRB participation.

No limitation should be placed on the ability of either party to bring disputes before the DRB, regardless of the alleged value of the dispute (often referred to as the magnitude of the quantum). The DRB has the responsibility to review all matters that are at an impasse following bilateral job-site negotiations.

Some specifications have limited the board's involvement to technical issues or to geotechnical considerations related to differing site conditions, as distinct from matters requiring the application or interpretation of the general and supplementary conditions and special provisions of the contract. An experienced DRB is at least as qualified to deal with these matters as are typical construction industry arbitrators, who commonly issue binding decisions an all contractual issues. Any distinction between a geotechnical or technical issue and a contract interpretation or legal issue should have no bearing on the activities of the DRB. Limiting jurisdiction can generate controversy over which disputes should go to the board.

2.2.3 Scope of Recommendations

Recommendations may be for entitlement only, for entitlement with guidelines for quantum, or for entitlement and quantum. The parties should agree on the type of recommendation desired. In case of disagreement, the board should exercise its judgment.

It is important that, well before the hearing, the board understands whether the entitlement and quantum issues are to be heard together or separately, so that the proper prehearing materials are exchanged between the parties and adequate time is allowed for the hearing.

When the parties disagree on the merit or entitlement aspects of a claim, a prompt recommendation from the board may assist the parties in analyzing the quantum issues. Such a step could save considerable time, since the quantum calculations need conform only to the agreed extent of the entitlements.

On the other hand, an owner may be reluctant to accept a DRB recommendation on entitlement in the fear that doing so will commit the owner to accepting an exorbitant claim for quantum. Knowing in advance what quantum the contractor expects will place the owner in a better position to evaluate the entitlement recommendation. Also, when the assessment of quantum is very complicated, it may be difficult for the DRB to structure a standalone entitlement recommendation without considering its impact on the quantum calculations.

Another possibility, therefore, is an entitlement recommendation that includes guidelines for quantum assessment. Once the board becomes aware of the details surrounding a dispute, it is in a good position to determine whether quantum guidelines would be beneficial. Then, either before or after referral of the dispute, the DRB can suggest that its deliberations include the issue of settlement guidelines.

Many disputes are rather simple. Examples include those involving an interpretation of certain provisions in the contract. The ensuing calculation of quantum may not require detailed review of cost records, and daily reports. In such cases, a DRB recommendation covering both entitlement and quantum might be most appropriate.

In other cases, the parties might agree on important factual matters involving quantum. For example, a detailed auditor's report on the contractor's cost records may be accepted by both parties. Other factual matters, such as labor time records, may be agreed to. Sometimes, the owner has prepared a detailed assessment of the contractor's calculations so the differences are readily identified. All these steps would simplify the work of the DRB.

Both parties should be aware of the ramifications involving the scope of a DRB recommendation. These should be freely discussed between the parties and with the board to arrive at a definite agreement on the scope of each action requested from the DRB.

2.2.3.1 Advisory Recommendations. The traditional DRB procedure involves the prompt submittal of a dispute to the board, the holding of a hearing, and the issuance of the DRB recommendation.

Frequently, the parties disagree as to how certain provisions in the contract should be applied to a particular dispute. If they knew how the DRB would rule on such an issue, they could structure their negotiations accordingly and, in effect, arrive at a final settlement on their own.

If an issue such as that described above is formally submitted to the DRB as a dispute, the parties are committed to the entire process. If a party does not accept the DRB recommendation, it may be difficult to resume negotiations. To overcome these objections, the DRB may be asked to give an informal advisory opinion.

Although such an approach may appear to violate the accepted DRB procedures, it is actually quite logical. The fundamental purpose of the DRB concept is to encourage the prompt resolution of disputes. So long as an advisory recommendation is aimed at accomplishing that objective and does not compromise any other DRB principle, it should not be discouraged.

The DRB should not accept a request for an advisory recommendation unless both parties agree. Also, it should be clear that such an action will not compromise any other recommendation of the DRB or its relationship with the parties. Such a recommendation is advisory only and does not require a formal acceptance or rejection from either party. Even though the recommendation may offer guidance on issues other than that which impelled its first use, the circumstances surrounding those other issues might be such that it would no longer be valid. The possibility must be made clear to both parties.

Keeping these precautions in mind, the use of advisory recommendations shows promise of further enhancing the utility of the DRB concept.

2.2.4 Mechanics of Referral

2.2.4.1 Letter of Referral to DRB Chairperson. Referral of a dispute to the board, by either the contractor or the owner, should be made by letter to the board chairperson, with copies to the other party and the other two board members. Sometimes the process may be expedited at the regular meeting through inquiries regarding potential referrals.

2.2.4.2 Scheduling the Hearing. Upon receipt of the dispute referral letter, the board chairperson should consult with the other two members, the contractor, and the owner to fix a date for the hearing. Normally, the hearing should take place at the earliest date which is convenient for all concerned. Allowance should be made for the time the parties will need for preparation. When a matter is not urgent or will not require lengthy deliberations, the hearing could be scheduled for the next regular board meeting. Again, the scheduling can often be done during the DRB meeting.

2.2.4.3 Documentation. Typically each party will compile supporting materials, such as correspondence, reports, and other records. Since much of this material will be identical for both parties, it should be combined into one folio for use by the parties and the board, both before and during the hearing. The folio is a significant convenience to the board, since the position documents of each party reference backup documents in the same place.

These documents should be arranged in a logical manner.

Each item should be identified by page number. The parties' position papers then readily reference selected documents.

Obviously, the complete compilation of the backup folio requires full cooperation of the parties. If either party introduces additional backup material after the folio is finalized, its effectiveness will be reduced. The parties can use the backup folio during preparation of their position papers, and copies will be distributed to the board along with the position papers.

Although the use of a folio as described above will expedite progress of the hearing and the deliberations of the board, the procedure is not always implemented. The DRB should bring up the subject whenever it receives a dispute referral letter. If the advantage to all parties is clearly explained, the folio may be used more often.

2.2.4.4 Position Papers. Before the meeting, each party should prepare and submit to the other party and the board a brief paper describing its position. The paper should concisely summarize the party's position, explain relevant factual information, and give the contractual justification. All arguments which the party intends to put forth during the hearing should be included. Supporting material in the backup folio may be referenced as needed.

2.3 Conduct of the Hearing

DRB hearings should be conducted in a manner that encourages openness, candor, and the thorough disclosure of all pertinent information having a bearing on the dispute. The board should formulate its procedures of operation, and modify them whenever appropriate, to accomplish this objective while ensuring that the hearing will proceed in an orderly and efficient manner. The DRB should be empowered to decide all procedures, including recesses, adjournments, and continuation of hearings.

2.3.1 Location and Facilities

Hearings may be conducted at any mutually accepted location that provides all the required facilities and access to necessary documentation. The job site is preferred because many of the hearing participants and necessary records are readily available at this location.

The owner or a representative (architect, engineer, or construction manager) usually arranges for the hearing room and necessary accessories. Otherwise, the chairperson of the DRB can handle this responsibility.

A typical hearing requires a meeting room large enough to accommodate 15 to 20 people. Participants are seated around a large table with sufficient space to lay out drawings. Marker boards or flipcharts are provided to facilitate illustration during testimony. Wall space to hang drawings, plots, or charts should be available. Video and computer monitors, overhead and slide projectors, and other equipment should be on hand for presentations. It is useful to have reproduction facilities nearby to facilitate copying and distribution of information developed during the hearing. Board members should sit together at one end of the table in position to see clearly any displays or visual aids.

2.3.2 Participation

The board should reach agreement with each party on who will participate in the hearing as well as who may attend as observers. Additional participants at the hearing may include subcontractors, consultants, and witnesses. In case of disagreement, the board should be empowered to make the final decision.

If counsel is requested by either party, the board will decide whether the parties may have lawyers participate in the hearing or simply act as observers. All participants and their roles at the hearing should be disclosed sufficiently in advance to allow the parties to make adequate preparation. Unless required by open meeting laws, media representatives should not be admitted to the hearing, since their attendance will inhibit open and candid discussion by the parties.

2.3.3 Format of the Hearing

No more than two disputes should be considered during one hearing. A day's hearing should not last longer than 6 hours, excluding breaks.

The format of the hearing should allow each party to present all relevant material. Generally, the claimant makes its presentation first, followed by the other party. Rebuttals are then heard, followed by questions by the board and further questions by the parties. Each party must be given ample opportunity to present its case and to question the other party. The board must be satisfied that all pertinent information has been presented and understood. Legal rules of evidence are not observed. Cross-examination is not permitted.

Hearing presentations may include position statements, documentary evidence, and visual aids. New information, such as special consultant reports or additional evidence, should be provided to all parties in advance. Surprise is contrary to the open, cooperative attitude sought in DRB hearings.

Generally, each board member takes individual notes during the hearing, so the services of a court reporter are not required. However, if one of the parties insists upon such service and is willing to bear the costs, the board may allow it. Audio or video recording is usually prohibited, since it tends to inhibit discussion.

During or after the hearing, the DRB may request further information, such as additional correspondence, daily field reports, and purchasing records. The request may necessitate additional hearings in order to consider and fully understand all the material. The hearings will not be closed until both parties have nothing more to add.

Board members should avoid questions that could be construed as favoring either party and should refrain from expressing opinions on the merit of any facet of the case.

2.3.4 Conclusion of the Hearing

Before the hearing is adjourned, and usually after all presentations and rebuttals have been made, the board should meet privately to discuss the extent of its forthcoming deliberations. At this point, it should be able to estimate how much time the deliberations will consume as well as the time required to prepare its formal recommendations. Sometimes, in the case of urgent issues, the board may present an oral recommendation immediately after final adjournment, or on the following day.

After this private meeting, the hearing is resumed and the board presents the schedule for its deliberations and the preparation and submittal of its recommendations. The DRB may also request specific documents or ask the parties to address certain issues in writing. The hearing is then formally adjourned.

2.4   Deliberation and Recommendation

2.4.1   Location

Board deliberations can be conducted at any convenient location. Care should be exercised to ensure privacy. If additional information or access to project records is needed, a site near the project location is appropriate.

2.4.2   Schedule

After final adjournment, the board meets privately to discuss the case and prepare an agenda for its deliberations and the drafting of its recommendations. If all three members have generally similar positions, the main effort will be directed toward composing the recommendations. If not, one or more sessions may be held to reconcile differences.

The board prepares a detailed schedule covering all anticipated steps to complete its deliberations and prepare its report. The schedule should take into account any other commitments of the individual members.

2.4.3   Deliberations

The board's deliberations have two basic objectives. The first is to achieve agreement, or a meeting of minds, on the various issues in the dispute. The second is to develop a format and compose the recommendations in such a fashion that the parties fully understand the reasoning of the board.

Depending on the complexity of the case and the availability of the individual members, the deliberations and the drafting of the recommendations may take place simultaneously in joint sessions. Often, they take place through the exchange of output by means of facsimile followed by telephone conferences. The chairperson should take the lead in organizing these activities and keeping them on schedule.

2.4.4 Additional Information or Assistance

If, during the deliberations, the need arises for additional information, such as copies of documents not in the possession of the board, a request may be made to either party with a copy to the other. The same procedure may be followed for access to the escrow documents, assistance from outside consultants or experts, and the like.

2.4.5 Recommendations

The board's recommendations should be based on the information presented by the parties and must be compatible with the provisions of the contract and applicable laws and regulations. Depending on the facts and circumstances, the board may wish to consider relevant industry practice and standards and other appropriate information. Individual notions of fairness or equity should be suppressed.

It is important that the recommendations convince both parties that the board considered all points raised in their presentations. Each party's position should be summarized to ensure that it is understood. Points accepted as well as those rejected should be identified. The board's logic and line of reasoning should be explained.

One board member is usually delegated to assemble the draft recommendations. For complex cases having several different issues, this work may be divided among the three members. Some DRB recommendations have been extremely brief, with little explanation. Others have been long and wordy, with pages of material having little relevance to the basic claim issues. Both of these extremes should be avoided.

The first-draft recommendation is circulated among the members for suggested revisions. This process is continued, with the wording of all elements carefully considered. A unanimous recommendation should be the goal. In practice, it is found that by thoroughly reviewing and exploring one another's perspective, the members nearly always reach a recommendation acceptable to all.

See Appendix D for a sample format of a recommendation and Appendix E for examples of brief recommendations.

2.4.6 Presentation

For simple disputes in which the board conducts the hearing, completes its deliberations, and prepares its recommendations in one brief time frame (say, 1 or 2 days), the recommendations can be presented directly to the parties. The parties may be given an opportunity to ask questions and seek clarification. There appears to be no particular advantage to presenting recommendations in person. For cases of any complexity, the parties will need some time to study the report before reaching any conclusions. When a report is not presented in person, the unsigned recommendations are first transmitted by facsimile, with the signed recommendations sent later by courier.

In factually complex situations, especially those that involve many documents, the board may wish to issue a draft of (1) its understanding of the positions of the parties and (2) a factual history.

2.4.7 Negotiation

When a party does not accept a DRB recommendation, the case can go on to other avenues for resolution. However, the parties frequently continue their negotiations using the DRB recommendation as a guide. In the vast majority of cases these subsequent negotiations are successful.

2.4.8 Reconsideration

The guide specification permits a DRB recommendation to be referred back to the board for clarification or reconsideration. One party may seek to present information not offered at the hearing or to assert an additional argument. Sometimes what was assumed to be agreement on a factual matter turns out to be incorrect, and clarification is needed. The standards and criteria for reconsideration should be set forth in the contract; if they are not, they should be enumerated by the board. Sometimes the parties have a legitimate basis for seeking clarification. Reconsideration should be the exception, not the rule. Rearguing the same issue on the same facts is not productive.

When the board feels that a request for reconsideration or clarification is meritorious and will likely lead to an acceptable resolution of the dispute, it will honor the request. Usually, an additional hearing is not needed. The board reviews any new information together with commentary from the parties and, if necessary, prepares a revised or clarified recommendation which responds to the matters raised.

3
International Applications

3.0 Introduction

This chapter provides a brief examination of the use of DRBs outside North America, and suggests certain points which may require special consideration when a DRB is part of an international project.

The first known use of a DRB on a construction project outside North America was on the El Cajon Hydroelectric Plant, built in Honduras between 1980 and 1986. The main feature of this project was the construction of the then-highest concrete dam in the Western Hemisphere.

The success of the DRB concept on this project is demonstrated by the fact that the work was completed with no claims referred to arbitration or litigation. Also, and perhaps more important, the success of the DRB at El Cajon stirred increased interest in the DRB concept at the World Bank. The Bank had long despaired of the difficulties facing its borrowers in resolving disputes on Bank-financed projects.

After El Cajon, there was for many years no recorded use of a DRB on an international contract. This point, as well as the more recent growing interest in the subject, is reviewed in the following paragraphs.

Chapter Three

3.1 Influence of FIDIC

The Fédération Internationale des Ingénieurs Conseils (FIDIC) publishes and periodically updates its *Conditions of Contract (International) for Works of Civil Engineering Construction.* These FIDIC provisions are used for international construction works, including those funded by the World Bank. The *Conditions of Contract* provide for an "engineer," separate from but retained by the "employer," to administer and supervise the construction of the project by the successful "tenderer" (the contractor). The status of the "engineer" under FIDIC may be contrasted with that of the "construction manager" often found in U.S. projects. The latter typically enters contracts on behalf of the owner or in general manages the project as an agent of the owner, so that with respect to DRB procedures it is synonymous with the owner. Under FIDIC, the engineer acts as a separate entity.

FIDIC Clause 67, entitled "Settlement of Disputes," is the one which vitally affects the use of a DRB. Under this clause, the engineer is responsible for settling disputes between the owner and the contractor as well as those between the engineer and the contractor. The engineer's decision is binding on both parties unless one of them refers to arbitration. This quasi-judicial role, even over matters involving the engineer's own actions, has been supported by a long tradition of strong professional independence among British consulting engineers, even on matters affecting the consulting engineer and its client. It must be noted that this tradition has resulted in a long and honorable history of successful resolution of disputes by both British engineers and engineers of other nationalities working under the FIDIC-style *Conditions of Contract.*

However, today this procedure has become increasingly unsatisfactory. More and more disputes in international contracts result in arbitration of ever-increasing duration and cost. As an employee of the owner, the engineer can hardly be expected to act with complete impartiality. This is especially true when the dispute is generated by some act or decision of the engineer. The problem is then grossly exacerbated by the extreme amount of time consumed. The engineer may take as much as the full 84 days allowed by FIDIC Clause 67 to publish his or her decision. After that, months will elapse before arbitration can be started. The arbitration itself often consumes many more months, if not years.

For this reason, contractors are very reluctant to request a decision from the engineer, even when, under most current DRB modifications to Clause 67, the DRB can be activated immediately after the engineer's decision is published. Whether there is a DRB or not, to request an engineer's decision places the contractor inexorably on the path to international arbitration. Contractors do not wish to take this path for every dispute which might surface during the performance of the work. If they must resort to arbitration, they prefer to do so after contract completion. Then, all the unresolved claims can be combined into one huge omnibus claim.

Of course, the answer to this dilemma is to allow the DRB to consider claims early on, as soon as it is apparent that the parties are not likely to resolve the dispute themselves. So far, under the current modifications to Clause 67, the engineer vigorously resists this sensible solution and the employer usually supports the engineer.

In the United States, the DRB is inserted as an intermediate step in the owner's existing dispute settlement procedures. In practice, this step is usually taken during the early stages of a dispute and the DRB recommendations are issued promptly. Usually that concludes the matter; if not, either party is then free to pursue other remedies. With FIDIC, this is not possible unless the engineer's role is modified. If the DRB is inserted before the engineer's decision is sought, the engineer's responsibility to settle the dispute and issue a written decision is abrogated. Or else the entire process is further delayed awaiting the decision, which would no doubt be needed to advise the employer whether to accept the DRB recommendation. If the formal engineer's decision is required after the DRB acts, the process loses the advantage of early resolution of the dispute.

It appears that this dilemma may have been instrumental in discouraging the use of DRBs on international construction contracts, with both employers and consulting engineering firms reluctant to change the role of the engineer in FIDIC Clause 67. Although the employer routinely modifies many of the FIDIC clauses to accommodate its circumstances and policies, the natural human propensity to maintain the status quo may account for failure to change Clause 67. In any case, several DRBs have recently been organized on international contracts, with the

DRB usually inserted after the engineer's decision. The results have not been encouraging.

If all parties are sincerely interested in seeing the DRB concept succeed, they can easily, either informally or by change order, expedite the process and overcome the objections outlined above. However, this step has rarely been taken. It seems obvious that Clause 67 must be modified to eliminate the engineer's role in dispute resolution and to provide for a DRB.

Fortunately, the World Bank is currently taking a landmark step in this direction. Although not officially published at this time, its *Sample Bidding Documents for Works* includes a modified FIDIC Clause 67. Under the modified clause, the engineer is relieved of any responsibility to settle disputes. Instead, disputes are to be referred quickly to the DRB. If either party is dissatisfied with the DRB recommendation, it is free to proceed to arbitration.

The Bank will require the use of a DRB on large projects. As of this writing, the exact amount to define a "large project" has not been determined, but would be in the range of $25 million to $100 million. For projects valued below this minimum, a DRB will not be mandatory, but will be strongly encouraged. These actions by the World Bank will provide a strong impetus to the movement to settle international construction disputes promptly at the job-site level.

A suggested revision of FIDIC Clause 67 and its Annex A is included at the end of this chapter. The revision is compatible with the current thinking at the World Bank.

The World Bank version of a DRB-modified FIDIC Clause 67 provides that if either party is dissatisfied with a recommendation of the board, it can prevent the recommendation from becoming binding only by giving notice, within 14 days, of its intention to commence arbitration. This provision appears to contradict the DRB concept of resolving small disputes before they grow out of control. Neither party wants to invoke international arbitration for a small dispute which might still be resolved through negotiations. There is nothing in the recommended clause to prevent the parties from postponing the arbitration to as late as project completion. However, it is suggested that the World Bank version be modified to specifically allow the parties to mutually defer the commencement of arbitration pending further attempts to resolve the dispute.

3.2 Other ADR Proposals

Along with the recent movement toward the use of DRBs on international construction contracts, several organizations are taking a step in that direction by advocating the involvement of a neutral third party in the dispute resolution process. This neutral party is variously called adjudicator, conciliator, expert, mediator, or referee. Some of the organizations participating in this movement are:

World Bank (for small works, under $50 million)

U.K. Institution of Civil Engineers (ICE)

Engineering Advancement Association of Japan (ENAA)

International Chamber of Commerce (ICC)

Fédération Internationale des Ingénieurs Conseils (FIDIC)

UN Commission on International Trade Law (UNICITRAL)

One example is the new engineering contract (NEC) published by ICE in 1993. The NEC provides for the appointment of a completely independent adjudicator to hear disputes promptly whenever so requested by the on-site representatives of the contractor and employer. The proposed adjudicator would be identified by the employer in the bidding documents. If the contractor does not agree, the two parties can mutually select an alternate.

All these concepts are indicative of a growing realization of the need for a better process for avoiding and resolving disputes. Nonetheless, they generally lack many of the unique virtues of the DRB. They are usually adopted after a dispute has arisen and thus lose the advantage of early involvement. They also lack the advantage of having three different viewpoints or perspectives, as is available in the DRB. Other organizations, such as the International Tunnelling Association, have also been studying various ADR methods and give prominence to the advantages and obvious success of the DRB concept.

3.3 Special Considerations

When a DRB is planned for an international construction contract, a number of key points need to be considered, and several provisions used in U.S. domestic contracts may need to be changed. These issues are discussed below.

3.3.1 Qualifications

3.3.1.1 Nationality. In addition to the usual professional and conflict-of-interest qualifications, special precautions should be taken to avoid the potential or even the perception of partiality. When it is deemed advisable, DRB members should not have the nationality of either the owner or the contractor (including joint-venture partners). Alternatively, only the board chairperson may be asked to comply with this restriction. On the other hand, one case studied for this manual required that all DRB members be nationals of the employer's country. How this works out in practice remains to be seen.

3.3.1.2 Language. All DRB members should be fluent in the language used in the contract documents and in the administration of the work. They should be able to prepare their recommendations in that language.

3.3.1.3 Indoctrination. All DRB members should have an understanding of the DRB concept requiring them to be completely independent of the parties and to serve both parties equally, equitably, and fairly.

3.3.2 Appointment

As in the United States, the first two DRB members are usually selected by the contracting parties, with each party approving the appointment of the other. The third member, or chairperson, is then selected by the first two members and is also approved by both parties.

In some cases, the first two DRB members are selected by an independent entity, such as the International Chamber of Commerce or the U.K. Institution of Civil Engineers. This procedure was used on one project to appoint a DRB to serve two separate contracts. However, independent selection runs the risk that one of the parties may not be satisfied with the appointments. The DRB concept requires that all parties be comfortable with all members of the DRB.

It is imperative that the DRB be organized early so it can meet on the site shortly after the work begins. Suggestions for expediting this objective include the requirement that the owner name one or more prospective appointees in the invitation to tender. Each tender would also include the names of one or more prospective appointees of the contractor. Each party could then approve (or select) one of the other's proposed appointees. In any case, the contract should impose time limits for the appointments and subsequent approvals. If any time limit is exceeded, the relevant appointment would be made by a specified independent entity.

Other suggested measures to avoid delay in organizing the DRB include a contract provision that a notice to proceed cannot be issued until the DRB is organized. Another would forbid any draw on the project loan until the DRB is in place.

3.3.3 Scope of Services

The DRB scope of services should cover all disputes of whatever nature that arise under the contract between the owner and the contractor. To include restrictions or specific categories within which the DRB can act is to risk circumventing the purpose of establishing the DRB.

One clause reviewed for this book provided for the parties to solicit an opinion from the DRB on a matter not needing a site visit. After the relevant documents were examined, a telephone conference would be held and the DRB would later submit an oral opinion. This innovation appears to be counterproductive. It increases the risk of misunderstandings and forgoes the advantage of exploring the dispute in person and enabling all views to be freely expressed. It is difficult to visualize such a dispute being so urgent that it could not await the next scheduled site visit.

The required conduct of the DRB is covered in the main body of this book. However, especially on international contracts in which the DRB has to travel long distances and usually remains on the site for about a week, it should be encouraged to pursue a proactive role. The board can offer discreet comments or advice on general matters so long as it does not compromise its position with respect to potential future disputes and does not infringe on the roles of the designer, engineer, or other consultants to the project. The DRB's role could include the issuance of an advisory recommendation, one that does not commit the parties or the board but that might be helpful in the resolution of a dispute. See Section 2.2.3.1 for more details.

3.3.4 Frequency of Visits

It would appear that some projects seek to reduce the cost of the DRB by placing a limit on the number of site visits, such as once every 6 months or even once a year. There is a risk of "false economy" in such an approach because the efficacy of the DRB obviously is related to its ability to maintain continuous familiarity with the project as it evolves. On most projects, a visit every 3 or 4 months is appropriate during the most active phases of the work. During less critical phases, the frequency can be reduced. The timing of the visits should be fixed by mutual agreement of the parties. Lacking such agreement, the DRB should decide.

The DRB should be specifically allowed to convene at any location of its own choosing for private meetings, such as for deliberations while preparing a recommendation on a dispute.

3.3.5 Compensation of DRB Members

On most domestic DRB projects, each member of the DRB negotiates his or her own fee structure. On international work, a consensus of those consulted for this manual is that all three members be paid fees at identical rates. These rates can be fixed at reasonable levels, considering the stature of the individuals involved.

Some clauses provide a fixed daily fee for all time spent traveling (with some reasonable maximum number of days per trip) together with time spent at the site or elsewhere on official business. In addition, a fixed monthly retainer fee is provided to compensate each member for maintaining availability, for the time spent reviewing documents at home, as well as for communications, clerical work, and other nontravel expenses. Without this retainer, provisions should be made to compensate the members for legitimate time and expenses incurred at home. Travel expenses are reimbursed at actual cost and first-class travel should be permitted. (It is noted that the World Bank will not fund first-class travel. Other arrangements might be made.)

The currency of payment must be specified. Payment in U.S. dollars is common, and is usually acceptable to all DRB members. Although there is no record of any problem with monetary exchange rates, under special circumstances consideration might be given to compensation for losses resulting from large exchange rate fluctuations between the currency of payment and that of the member's home country.

The spirit of the DRB concept requires that the owner and the contractor share all DRB fees and expenses equally. In many cases, the contractor pays the DRB invoices and then charges the owner for 50 percent. In other cases, each DRB member separately invoices each party for 50 percent.

The DRB three-party agreement should provide for the parties to bear the cost of any taxes or other levies against the DRB members' compensation, except those imposed in their home countries.

3.3.6 Liability

As with members of domestic DRBs, international board members should be absolved of any personal or professional liability arising from the activities and recommendations of the board.

3.3.7 Applicable Law, Personal Jurisdiction, and Venue

The three-party agreement among the owner, contractor, and dispute review board should clearly define what law is applicable to the agreement and what body or bodies are available to enforce any right or obligation under it. Also, there should be a provision defining how disputes between the contracting parties are to be resolved before legal action can be taken. The clauses reviewed for this manual prescribe private arbitration.

3.3.8 Recommendations of the Board

The recommendations of the DRB should be in writing and should clearly describe the board's reasoning in reaching its conclusions. Obviously, the board should frame its recommendations so that both parties, even though they may not accept them, will clearly understand the board's logic and the steps it took to arrive at its conclusions. This is especially true in countries where the DRB concept is new and the parties do not fully appreciate how the process works. It is best to avoid long, wordy narratives on issues which may not be exactly germane to the particular facets of the dispute. The DRB process is not a judicial proceeding, and studious logistic opinions are not appropriate. Nevertheless, all recommendations must concisely explain the reasons behind them and the procedures for implementing them.

The three-party agreement should state that the board make every effort to reach a unanimous decision, which would carry more weight than a split decision. Experience has shown that when DRB deliberations begin, there may be a wide diversity of positions. However, after thoroughly reviewing the facts and the evidence, the three members nearly always are able to reach a unanimous recommendation which is satisfactory to all. However, the DRB provisions should not demand a unanimous decision, since that would impinge upon the board members' independent expert judgment.

The DRB provisions should also stipulate that in case of any subsequent arbitral or court proceeding, the recommendations of the board are admissible as evidence. This is a powerful motivation for the owner and the contractor to accept the recommendations. Even if the recommendations are not accepted, they can assist in expediting the conclusion of such subsequent proceedings. The members of the board should not be barred from giving evidence in such proceedings.

3.3.9 Alternate DRB Members

One of the clauses examined for this manual provided for alternate DRB members to be appointed in any dispute. In the event that a principal DRB member is unable to participate, an alternate could be used. This approach may have superficial appeal, but it poses inherent difficulties because of the alternate's lack of familiarity with the progress of the work throughout construction and possible lack of familiarity with the other DRB members. Thus, it seems preferable to defer consideration of a dispute rather than to employ alternates. Permanent inability of a DRB member to serve can be dealt with under the replacement procedures established in the DRB agreement.

3.3.10 Blocking Attempts

In a few DRB cases, one party has deliberately attempted to circumvent the activities of the board. Such a move would probably leave the other party in the position of being able to allege breach of contract, but meanwhile the DRB mechanism remains inoperative.

No clauses studied for this book revealed any attempts to empower a DRB to proceed without the participation of one of the parties, a situation that is true for some methods of institutional arbitration. No doubt this is because the essence of the DRB concept requires voluntary cooperation of the parties. Nevertheless, once a dispute is referred to the DRB in strict conformance with the contract, the board should be empowered to decide how the hearing and other steps are conducted. It should retain full control of the situation until its recommendations have been rendered and the parties have either accepted or rejected them.

Every effort should be made to anticipate possible ways in which the procedure could become stalled or inadvertently deadlocked and to evade as many blocking mechanisms as possible. Some potential problem areas are described below.

3.3.10.1 Resignations. Some fear has been expressed that a party which does not really wish to have the DRB mechanism in operation might seek to frustrate its functioning by arranging for a nominee to resign as soon as any dispute is put before the DRB. Following the renomination and approval procedure, presumably the same act would be repeated. The consensus of those assisting in this manual is that if DRB members of international repute are selected, it is unlikely that they would agree to any such arrangement.

3.3.10.2 Replacement. Of course, it is possible to have a resignation in good faith or a requirement to replace a member for some other reason. The mechanism for a replacement is an essential element of the agreement establishing the DRB and of the agreement with DRB members. Those clauses which deal with these points typically provide that replacements be selected in the same way as the original nominees. Also, it is advisable to state that failure to provide a replacement within specified time limits will allow either party to obtain a replacement by an independent and impartial third party, such as the secretary general of ICSID.

3.3.10.3 Postponement of Meetings or Hearings. One party, usually the employer, may offer some excuse to continuously postpone a DRB meeting. Since it is recommended that the DRB specifically have the authority to fix the timing of meetings when the parties cannot agree, such an attempt can be thwarted. The DRB should not permit an unreasonable use of this ploy.

3.3.10.4 Nonpayment to Board Members. The contractor may attempt to block the proceedings by failing to make payment. Or the owner may fail to reimburse the contractor for its share of the payment. One method of preventing such maneuvers is to include a provision that enables one party to make payment on behalf of the defaulting party. Such payment would then contractually create a debt due from the defaulting party. The contract or three-party agreement should specifically state that failure of either party to make payment as provided shall constitute a default with respect to the construction contract.

The following is author A. A. Mathews' suggested modification to FIDIC Subclause 67.1 and Annex A. The World Bank will shortly issue a final version of this clause, which may have further modifications.

[Conditions of Particular Application]

Clause 67—Settlement of Disputes

Sub-Clause 67.1: Dispute Review Board. Subclause 67.1 is modified to read as follows:

If a dispute of any kind whatsoever arises between the Employer and the Contractor in connection with, or arising out of, the Contract or the execution of the Works, whether during the execution of the Works or after their completion and whether before or after the repudiation or other termination of the Contract, including any disagreement by either party with any action, inaction, opinion, instruction, determination, certificate, or valuation of the Engineer, the matter in dispute shall, in the first place, be referred to the Dispute Review Board ("the Board").

The Board shall be established by the signing of a Board Member's Declaration of Acceptance (as required by paragraph 12 of Annex A to these Conditions of Particular Application) by all three Board Members.

The Board shall comprise three Members experienced with the type of construction involved in the Works and with the interpretation of contractual documents. One Member shall be selected by each of the Employer and the Contractor and approved by the other. If either of these Members is not so selected and approved within 28 days of the date of the Letter of Acceptance, then upon the request of either or both parties such Member shall be selected within 14 days of such request by the Chairman of the International Court of Arbitration of the International Chamber of Commerce, Paris. The third Member shall be selected by the other two and approved by the parties.

If the two Members selected by or on behalf of the parties fail to select the third Member within 14 days after the later of their selections, or if within 14 days after the selection of the third Member the parties fail to approve that Member, then upon the request of either or both parties such third Member shall be selected promptly by the Chairman of the International Court of Arbitration of the International Chamber of Commerce, Paris, who shall seek the approval of the proposed third Member by the parties before selection but, failing such approval, nevertheless shall select the third Member. The third Member shall serve as Chairman of the Board.

In the event of death, disability, or resignation of any Member, such Member shall be replaced in the same manner as the Member being replaced was selected. If for whatever other reason a Member shall fail or be unable to serve, the Chairman (or failing the action of the Chairman then either of the other Members) shall inform the parties and such non-serving Member shall be replaced in the same manner as the Member being replaced was selected. Any replacement made by the parties shall be completed with 28 days after the event giving rise to the vacancy on the Board, failing which, the replacement shall be made by the Chairman of the International Court of Arbitration of the International Chamber of Commerce, Paris, in the same manner as described above. Replacement shall be considered completed when the new Member signs the Board Member's Declaration of Acceptance. Throughout any replacement process the Members not being replaced shall continue to serve and the Board shall continue to function and its activities shall have the same force and effect as if the vacancy had not occurred, provided however, that the Board shall not conduct a hearing nor issue a Recommendation until the replacement is completed.

Either the Employer or the Contractor may refer a dispute to the Board in accordance with the provisions of Annex A to these Conditions of Particular Application.

If either the Employer or the Contractor is dissatisfied with any Recommendation of the Board, or if the Board fails to issue its Recommendation within the time limit specified in Annex A, Par. 9(f), then either the Employer or the Contractor may, within 14 days after his receipt of the Recommendation, or within 14 days after the expiry of the said time limit, as the case may be, give notice to the other party, with a copy for information to the Engineer, of his intention to commence arbitration, as hereinafter provided, as to the matter in dispute. Such notice shall establish the entitlement of the party giving the same to commence arbitration, as hereinafter provided, as to such dispute and, subject to Sub-Clause 67.4, no arbitration in respect thereof may be commenced unless such notice is given.

If the Board has issued a Recommendation to the Employer and the Contractor within 28 days after its final hearing on the dispute and no notice of intention to commence arbitration as to such dispute has been given by either the Employer or the Contractor within 14 days after the parties received such Recommendation from the Board, the Recommendation shall become final and binding upon the Employer and the Contractor.

Whether or not it has become final and binding upon the Employer and the Contractor, a Recommendation shall be admissible as evidence in any subsequent dispute resolution procedure, including any arbitration or litigation having any relation to the dispute to which the Recommendation relates.

All Recommendations which have become final and binding shall be implemented by the parties forthwith, such implementation to include any relevant action of the Engineer.

Unless the Contract has already been repudiated or terminated, the Contractor shall, in every case, continue to proceed with the Works with all due diligence and the Contractor and the Employer shall give effect forthwith to every decision of the Engineer unless and until the same shall be revised as a result of the operation of this Sub-Clause 67.1 or, as hereinafter provided, in an arbitral award.

Sub-Clause 67.2.   Sub-Clause 67.2 is deleted without a change in the numbering of the other Sub-Clauses of this Clause 67.

Sub-Clause 67.3: Arbitration.   Sub-Clause 67.3 is modified to read as follows:

Any dispute in respect of which the Recommendation, if any, of the Board has not become final and binding shall be finally settled by arbitration under the Rules of Conciliation and

Arbitration of the International Chamber of Commerce by one or more arbitrators appointed under such Rules. The arbitral tribunal shall have full power to open up, review, and revise any decision, opinion, instruction, determination, certificate, or valuation of the Engineer and any Recommendation(s) of the Board related to the dispute.

Neither party shall be limited in the proceedings before such tribunal to the evidence or arguments put before the Board for the purpose of obtaining its Recommendation(s) pursuant to Sub-Clause 67.1. No Recommendation shall disqualify any Board Member from being called as a witness and giving evidence before the arbitrator(s) on any matter whatsoever relevant to the dispute.

Arbitration may be commenced prior to or after completion of the Works, provided that the obligations of the Employer, the Engineer, the Contractor, and the Board shall not be altered by reason of the arbitration being conducted during the progress of the Works.

The appointing authority shall be the International Chamber of Commerce. The place of arbitration shall be London, England, and the language of arbitration shall be English.

Sub-Clause 67.4: Failure to Comply with Recommendation. Sub-Clause 67.4 is amended to read as follows:

Where neither the Employer nor the Contractor has given notice of intention to commence arbitration of a dispute within the period stated in Sub-Clause 67.1 and the related Recommendation has become final and binding, either party may, if the other party fails to comply with such Recommendation and without prejudice to any other right it may have, refer the failure to arbitration in accordance with Sub-Clause 67.3. The provisions of Sub-Clause 67.1 shall not apply to any such reference.

Annex A to
[Conditions of Particular Application]

Dispute Review Board's Rules and Procedures

1. Except for providing the services required hereunder, the Board Members shall not give any advice to either party or to the Engineer concerning conduct of the Works. The Board Members:

(a) shall have no financial interest in any party to the Contract, or the Engineer; or a financial interest in the Contract, except for payment for services on the Board;

(b) shall have had no previous employment by, or financial ties to, any party to the Contract, or the Engineer, except for fee-based consulting services on other projects, all of which must be disclosed in writing to both parties prior to appointment to the Board;

(c) shall have disclosed in writing to both parties prior to appointment to the Board any and all recent or close professional or personal relationships with any director, officer, or employee of any party to the Contract, or the Engineer, and any and all prior involvement in the project to which the Contract relates;

(d) shall not, while a Board Member, be employed whether as a consultant or otherwise by either party to the Contract, or the Engineer, except as a Board Member, without the prior consent of the parties and the other Board Members;

(e) shall not, while a Board Member, engage in discussion or make any agreement with any party to the Contract, or with the Engineer, regarding employment whether as a consultant or otherwise either after the Contract is completed or after service as a Board Member is completed;

(f) shall be and remain impartial and independent of the parties and shall disclose in writing to the Employer, the Contract, the Engineer, and one another any fact or circumstance which might be such as to cause either the Employer or the Contractor to question the continued existence of the impartiality and independence required of Board Members; and

(g) shall be fluent in the language of the Contract.

2. Except for its participation in the Board's activities as provided in the Contract and in this Agreement, none of the Employer, the Contractor, and/or the Engineer shall solicit advice or consultation from the Board or the Board Members on matters dealing with the conduct of the Works.

3. The Employer shall:

(a) Furnish to each Board Member one copy of all documents which the Board may request, including Contract Documents, progress reports, variation orders, and other documents pertinent to the performance of the Contract.

(b) In cooperation with the Contractor, coordinate the Site visits of the Board, including conference facilities, and secretarial and copying services.

4. The Board shall begin its activities following the signing of a Board Member's Declaration of Acceptance by all three Board Members, and it shall terminate these activities as set forth below:

(a) The Board shall terminate its regular activities when either (i) the Defects Liability Period referred to in Sub-Clause 49.1 has expired, or (ii) the Employer has expelled the Contractor from the Site pursuant to Sub-Clause 63.1, and when in either case, the Board has communicated to the parties and the Engineer its Recommendations on all disputes previously referred to it.

(b) Once the Board has terminated its regular activities as provided by the previous paragraph, the Board shall remain available to process any dispute referred to it by either party. In case of such a referral, Board members shall receive payments as provided in paragraphs 7(a)(ii), (iii), and (iv).

5. Board Members shall not assign or subcontract any of their work under these Rules and Procedures.

6. The Board Members are independent contractors and not employees or agents of either the Employer or the Contractor.

7. Payments to the Board Members for their services shall be governed by the following provisions:

(a) Each Board Member will receive payments as follows:

(i) A retainer fee per calendar month equivalent to three times the daily fee established as of the date of Contract Award for arbitrators under the Administrative and Financial Regulations of the International Center for Settlement of Investment Disputes (the ICSID Arbitrator's Daily Fee), or such other retainer as the Employer and Contractor may agree in writing. This retainer shall be considered as payment in full for:

    (A) Being available, on reasonable notice, for all hearings, Site visits, and other meetings of the Board.

    (B) Being conversant with all project developments and maintaining relevant files.

    (C) All office and overhead expenses such as secretarial services, photocopying, and office supplies (but not including telephone calls, faxes, and telexes) incurred in connection with the duties as a Board Member.

    (D) All services performed hereunder except those performed during the days referred to in paragraph (ii) below.

  (ii) A daily fee equivalent to the ICSID Arbitrator's Daily Fee, or such other daily fee as the Employer and Contractor may agree in writing. This daily fee shall only be payable in respect to the following days, and shall be considered as payment in full for:

    (A) Each day up to a maximum of two days of travel time in each direction for the journey between the Board Member's home and the Site or other location of a Board meeting.

    (B) Each day on Site or other locations of a Board meeting.

  (iii) Expenses. In addition to the above, all reasonable and necessary travel expenses (including less than first-class airfare, subsistence, and other direct travel expenses) as well as the cost of telephone calls, faxes, and telexes incurred in connection with the duties as Board Member shall be reimbursed against invoices. Receipts for all expenses in excess of US $25.00 (US Dollars Twenty-Five) shall be provided.

  (iv) Reimbursement of any taxes that may be levied in the country of the Site on payments made to the Board Member (other than a national or permanent resident of the country of the Site) pursuant to this paragraph 7.

(b) Escalation. The retainer and fees shall remain fixed for the period of each Board Member's term.

(c) Phasing out of monthly retainer fee. Beginning with the next month after the Taking Over Certificate referred to in Clause 48 (not including any Portion Certificates issued under Clause 48.1A) has been issued, the Board Members shall receive only one-third of the monthly retainer fee. Beginning with the next month after the Board has terminated its regular activities pursuant to paragraph 4(a) above, the Board Members shall no longer receive any monthly retainer fee.

(d) Payments to the Board Members shall be shared equally by the Employer and the Contractor. The Contractor shall pay Members' invoices within 30 calendar days after receipt of such invoices and shall invoice the employer (through the monthly statements to be submitted in accordance with Sub-Clause 60.1 of the General Conditions) for one-half of the amounts of such invoices. The Employer shall pay such Contractor's invoices within the time period specified in the Construction Contract for other payments to the Contractor by the Employer.

(e) Failure of either the Employer or the Contractor to make payment in accordance with this Agreement shall be a fundamental breach of the Construction Contract, constituting an event of default under the Construction Contract, entitling the nondefaulting party to take the measures set forth in the Construction Contract for events of default.

(f) Notwithstanding such event of default, and without waiver of rights therefrom, in the event that either the Employer or the Contractor fails to make payment in accordance with these Rules and Procedures, the other party may pay whatever amount may be required to maintain the operation of the Board. The party making such payments, in addition to all other rights arising from such default, shall be entitled to reimbursement of all sums paid in excess of one-half of the amount required to maintain operation of the Board, plus all costs of obtaining such sums.

8. Board Site Visits:

(a) The Board shall visit the Site and meet with representatives of the Employer and the Contractor and the Engineer at regular intervals, at times of critical construction events, and at the written request of either party. As long as significant work is being performed, Site visits shall average at least once every four months. The timing of Site visits shall be as agreed among the Employer, the Contractor and the Board, but failing agreement, shall be fixed by the Board.

(b) Site visits shall include an informal discussion of the status of the construction of the Works, an inspection of the Works, and a review of the status of all potential and pending claims, including any Requests for Recommendation made or to be made in accordance with paragraph 9 below. Site visits shall be attended by personnel from the Employer, the Contractor, and the Engineer.

(c) At the conclusion of each Site visit, the Board shall prepare a report covering its activities during the visit and shall send copies to the parties and to the Engineer.

9. Procedure for Dispute Referral to the Board:

(a) If either party objects to any action or inaction of the other party or the Engineer, the objecting party may file a written Notice of Dispute to the other party with a copy to the Engineer stating that it is given pursuant to Clause 67 and stating clearly and in detail the basis of the dispute.

(b) The party receiving the Notice of Dispute will consider it and respond in writing within 14 days after receipt.

(c) This response shall be final and conclusive on the subject, unless a written appeal to the response is filed with the responding party within 7 days after receiving the response. Both parties are encouraged to pursue the matter further to attempt to settle the dispute. When it appears that the dispute cannot be resolved without the assistance of the Board, or if the party receiving the Notice of Dispute fails to provide a written response within 14 days after receipt of such Notice, either party may refer the dispute to the Board by written Request for Recommendation to the Board. The Request shall be addressed to the Chairman of the Board, with copies to the other Board Members, the other party, and the Engineer, and it shall state that it is made pursuant to Clause 67.

(d) The Request for Recommendation shall state clearly and in full detail the specific issues of the dispute to be considered by the Board.

(e) When a dispute is referred to the Board, and the Board is satisfied that the dispute requires the Board's assistance, the Board shall decide when to conduct a hearing on the dispute. The Board may request that written documentation and arguments from both parties be submitted to each Board Member before the hearing begins. The parties shall submit, insofar as possible, agreed statement of the relevant facts.

(f) During the hearing, the Contractor, the Employer, and the Engineer shall each have ample opportunity to be heard and to offer evidence. The Board's Recommendations for resolution of the dispute will be given in writing to the Employer, the Contractor, and the Engineer as soon as possible, and in any event not less than 28 days after the Board's final hearings on the dispute, or such other time as agreed by the parties and the Board.

10. Conduct of Hearing:

(a) Normally, hearings will be conducted at the Site, but any location that would be more convenient and still provide all required facilities and access to necessary documentation may be utilized by the Board. Private sessions of the Board may be held at any cost-effective location convenient to the Board.

(b) The Employer, the Engineer, and the Contractor shall be given the opportunity to have representatives at all hearings.

(c) During the hearings, no Board Member shall express any opinion concerning the merit of the respective arguments of the parties.

(d) After the hearings are concluded, the Board shall meet privately to formulate its Recommendations. All Board deliberations shall be conducted in private, with all Members' individual views kept strictly confidential. The Board's

Recommendations, together with an explanation of its reasoning, shall be submitted in writing to both parties and to the Engineer. The Recommendations shall be based on the pertinent Contract provisions, applicable laws and regulations, and the facts and circumstances involved in the dispute.

(e) The Board shall make every effort to reach a unanimous Recommendation. If this proves impossible, the majority shall decide, and the dissenting Member may prepare a written minority report for submission to both parties and to the Engineer.

11. In all procedural matters, including the furnishing of written documents and arguments relating to disputes, Site visits, and conduct of hearings, the Board shall have full and final authority.

12. After having been selected and, where necessary, approved, each Board Member shall sign two copies of the following declaration and make one copy available each to the Employer and to the Contractor:

BOARD MEMBER'S DECLARATION OF ACCEPTANCE

WHEREAS

(a) a Construction Contract (the Contract) for the _____
_____ has been signed on (date: _____
_____) between _____
_____ (the Employer) and _____
_____ (the Contractor);

(b) Clause 67 of the Conditions of Particular Application of the Construction Contract and Annex A to said Conditions provide for the establishment and operation of a Dispute Review Board (the Board);

(c) the undersigned has been selected (and where required, approved) to serve as a Board Member on said Board;

NOW THEREFORE, the undersigned Board Member hereby declares as follows:

1. I accept the selection as a Board Member and agree to serve on the Board and to be bound by the provisions of Clause 67 of the Conditions of Particular Application of the Contract and Annex A to said Conditions.

2. With respect to paragraph 1 of said Annex A, I declare:

(a) that I have no financial interest of the kind referred to in subparagraph (a);
(b) that I have had no previous employment or financial ties of the kind referred to in subparagraph (b); and
(c) that I have made to both parties any disclosures that may be required by subparagraphs (b) and (c).

BOARD MEMBER:

_____

Date: _____

Appendix **A**

Tabulation of Dispute Review Boards

Introduction

The DRB process has proved itself beyond all expectations. Almost $7 billion of construction has been completed using DRBs, and the record as of January 1994 is perfect; no disputes submitted to a DRB have been litigated.

In terms of dollar value, the growth of DRB use around the world is compounding at 50 percent a year. Total value of completed, ongoing, and planned projects with DRBs is now $22 billion.

On the 68 completed projects tabulated in this appendix, over 120 recommendations for settlements have been made and accepted. Many of these were major disputes that, without the DRB process, would have resulted in litigation. Equally impressive is the belief, on most of these projects, that the mere presence of the DRB was instrumental in avoiding additional disputes. These completed contracts comprised almost $3 billion worth of construction.

In addition to the 68 completed projects, DRBs are functioning on 98 ongoing projects and are planned for another 162 projects. On jobs under construction, 88 disputes have been settled.

In 1993, it was expected that DRBs would be used on 60 percent of the tunnel and underground projects bid in the United

States, representing over 70 percent of the dollar value. The California, Colorado, Maine, Hawaii, Massachusetts, and Washington Departments of Transportation are using DRBs. Washington DOT has completed 20 DRB projects, and now has another 12 under construction.

After experiencing extensive claims on their subway construction, both the Los Angeles and Washington, DC metros will use DRBs on all remaining tunnel and station contracts. Toronto will use DRBs on its metro expansion contracts. The Bay Area Rapid Transit (BART) is using DRBs on its extension contracts.

DRBs are spreading around the world and are now in use in China, India, South Africa, and Lesotho and are slated to be used in Bangladesh.

The accompanying summary table shows the record of all DRBs known to the authors as of January 1994. Corrections, additions, and updates are solicited. As can be seen in the table, the fastest growth of DRB use is now in building and process plant construction. The following owners have used DRBs on building and process contracts:

American Telephone & Telegraph

City of Akron

City of Anchorage

Central Contra Costa County Sanitary District

City of Fresno

Hawaii Department of Transportation

International Monetary Fund

Los Angeles County

Philadelphia Convention Authority

City of Phoenix

Texas Department of Criminal Justice

University of Washington

CUMULATIVE SUMMARY

	TO JANUARY 1988			TO FEBRUARY 1991			TO JANUARY 1994				INCREASE 91 TO 94			INCREASE 91 TO 94		
	EACH	$ B	DISPUTES SETTLED	EACH	$ B	DISPUTES SETTLED	EACH	$ B	DISPUTES SETTLED	DISPUTES SETTLED PER CONTRACT	EACH	$ B	DISPUTES SETTLED	EACH	$ B	DISPUTES SETTLED
COMPLETED CONTRACTS																
TUNNELS & UNDERGROUND	4	0.2	6	11	0.3	10	29	1.0	36	1.2	18	1	26	164%	272%	260%
HEAVY - HIGHWAY	2	0.3	9	7	0.5	40	31	1.2	72	2.3	24	1	32	343%	141%	80%
BUILDING & PROCESS	1	0.5	0	3	0.3	13	8	0.5	15	1.9	5	0	2	167%	70%	15%
TOTALS	7	0.9	15	21	1.1	63	68	2.7	123	1.8	47	2	60	224%	153%	95%
CONTRACTS UNDER CONSTRUCTION																
TUNNELS & UNDERGROUND	9	0.3	1	20	1.3	7	34	2.9	24	0.7	14	2	17	70%	126%	243%
HEAVY - HIGHWAY	3	0.2	0	21	0.8	8	43	2.9	55	1.3	22	2	47	105%	281%	588%
BUILDING & PROCESS	0	0.0	0	1	0.1	0	21	1.2	9	0.4	20	1	9	2000%	INF	INF
TOTALS	12	0.4	1	42	2.1	15	98	7.0	88	0.9	56	5	73	133%	229%	487%
CONTRACTS COMPLETE & UNDER CONSTRUCTION																
TUNNELS & UNDERGROUND	13	0.5	7	31	1.5	17	63	3.8	60	1.0	32	2	43	103%	151%	253%
HEAVY - HIGHWAY	5	0.5	9	28	1.3	48	74	4.1	127	1.7	46	3	79	164%	225%	165%
BUILDING & PROCESS	1	0.5	0	4	0.4	13	29	1.7	24	0.8	25	1	11	625%	335%	85%
TOTALS	19	1.4	16	63	3.2	78	166	9.7	211	1.3	103	7	133	163%	204%	171%
CONTRACTS PLANNED																
TUNNELS & UNDERGROUND	7	0.4	—	42	2.5	—	63	4.7	—	—	21	2	—	50%	91%	—
HEAVY - HIGHWAY	7	0.3	—	3	0.8	—	76	3.6	—	—	73	3	—	2433%	366%	—
BUILDING & PROCESS	0	0.0	—	0	0.0	—	33	0.9	—	—	33	1	—	INF	INF	—
TOTALS	14	0.7	—	45	3.2	—	172	9.2	—	—	127	6	—	282%	183%	—
ALL CONTRACTS																
TUNNELS & UNDERGROUND	20	0.9	7	73	4.0	17	126	8.5	60	—	53	5	43	73%	114%	253%
HEAVY - HIGHWAY	12	0.8	9	31	2.1	48	150	7.8	127	—	119	6	79	384%	278%	165%
BUILDING & PROCESS	1	0.5	0	4	0.4	13	62	2.6	24	—	58	2	11	1450%	547%	85%
TOTALS	33	2.1	16	108	6.4	78	338	18.9	211	—	230	12	133	213%	193%	171%

COMPLETED CONTRACTS

TUNNELS & UNDERGROUND

PROJECT NAME AND LOCATION	YEARS	OWNER	CONTRACTOR	TUNNEL DESCRIPTION LENGTH feet	DIAMETER feet	COST $ million	KEY	DISPUTES HEARD	SETTLED	LITIGATED
Eisenhower Tunnel, 2nd Bore Loveland Pass, CO	1975 1979	Colorado DOT	Kiewit	8,900	34	106	A	4	4	0
Mount Baker Ridge Tunnel, I-90 Seattle	1982 1986	Washington DOT	Atkinson	31,968 (1 at 1,332 ft x 63 ft)	x 9	36	A	3	3	0
Chambers Creek Interceptor Tacoma, WA	1983 1984	Pierce County	Mole Construction	11,700	6	10	AC	0	0	0
Hanging Lake Explor. Tunnel Glenwood Springs, CO	1983 1984	Colorado DOT	Shank-Artukovich	3,950	13	2	A	1	1	0
Beavertail Tunnel DeBeque, CO	1985 1987	Colorado DOT	Morrison-Knudsen	two at 600	43	18	HC	0	0	0
Metro Bus Tunnel Seattle	1987 1988	Seattle Metro	Atkinson-Dillingham	two at 4,100	20	45	YC	0	0	0
Sewer Relief, Increment 2 Honolulu	1987 1989	Honolulu City & Co	Kumagai Hawaii	5,200	5	10	A	0	0	0
Sewer Relief, Increment 3 Honolulu	1987 1989	Honolulu City & Co	Kumagai Hawaii	3,800	5	6	A	3	3	0
Westlake & Convention Sta Seattle	1987 1989	Seattle Metro	SCI Contractors	Cut & Cover Transit Stations		87	A	0	0	0
Sewer Relief, Increment 4 Honolulu	1987 1990	Honolulu City & Co	Pan Pacific Tokyu	5,400	5	11	A	0	0	0
San Antonio Channel Tunnels San Antonio, TX	1987 1993	Corps of Engineers	Ohbayashi	22,000	23	71	SY	13	13	0
Reverse Curve Tunnel Glenwood Canyon, CO	1988 1989	Colorado DOT	Shea	600	42	7	A	1	1	0
Bradley Lake Power Tunnel and Dam, Homer, AK	1988 1992	Alaska Power Authority	Ensearch Alaska	17,600	14	85	DC	0	0	0
Stanley Canyon Hydro Tunnel Colorado Springs, CO	1988 1993	City of Colo Spr	National Projects	17,500	9	32	AC	2	2	0

PROJECT NAME AND LOCATION	YEARS	OWNER	CONTRACTOR	DESCRIPTION	COST $ million	KEY	DISPUTES HEARD	SETTLED	LITIGATED
H-3 Exploratory Tunnel Honolulu	1989 1990	Hawaii DOT	Coluccio	7,000	13	A	1	1	0
Lehigh Tunnel No. 2 Allentown, PA	1989 1991	PA Turnpike Commission	Newberg Joint Venture	4,500	38	AC	0	0	0
State-Mount Hope System Rochester, NY	1989 1991	Monroe County	Grow & Conduit	8,000	29	A	0	0	0
Shot Tower Line, NE-01-01 Baltimore, MD	1989 1993	Baltimore Metro Trans	Kiewit/Shea	two at 5700	70	A	4	4	0
Hanging Lake Tunnel Glenwood Cyn, CO	1989 1994	Colorado DOT	Hanging Lake Joint Venture	two at 4,000	68	AC	0	0	0
Hemlock Tunnel Rehab Rochester, NY	1990 1991	City of Rochester	Hall Contracting	12,100	5	A	1	1	0
Trans-Missouri River Tunnel Kansas City, MO	1990 1992	City of Kansas City	Mole-Kassouf	14,600	21	A	0	0	0
Johns Hopkins, NE-02-02 Baltimore, MD	1990 1992	Baltimore Metro Trans	Kiewit/Shea	two at 700	13	A	1	1	0
H-3 Windward (Haiku) Tunnels Honolulu	1990 1993	Hawaii DOT	Frontier-Kemper, Traylor, Black	two at 3,500	108	A	1	1	0
Cowles Mountain Tunnel San Diego, CA	1991 1993	San Diego Co Water Auth	Traylor	6,800	11	A	1 Negotiations in progress	0	0
Deer Is. North Systems Tunnels Boston, MA	1991 1993	MA Water Res Auth	Kiewit, Atkinson, Kenny	9,050	20	D	1 One dispute to hear	1	0
SSC, N15-20 Ellis County, TX	1992 1993	DOE	Obayashi & Dillingham	14,300	18	A	0	0	0
SSC, N20-25 Ellis County, TX	1992 1993	DOE	Traylor Bros. Frontier-Kemper	12,700	14	A	0	0	0
SSC, N25-40 Ellis County, TX	1992 1993	DOE	Gilbert-Shea	43,700	16	A	0	0	0
SSC, N40-55 Ellis County, TX	1992 1993	DOE	Gilbert-Shea	44,900	12	A	0	0	0
TOTALS, COMPLETED TUNNELS & UNDERGROUND				29 EACH	$1.0 BILLION		37	36	0

HEAVY - HIGHWAY

PROJECT NAME AND LOCATION	YEARS	OWNER	CONTRACTOR	DESCRIPTION	COST $ million	KEY	DISPUTES HEARD	SETTLED	LITIGATED
Eisenhower Tunnel, 2nd Bore Loveland Pass, Colorado	1979 1981	Colorado DOT	Weaver Construction	Finish work in Tunnel	15	A	12	12	0
El Cajon Hydro Project Honduras	1980 1986	ENEE	Impregilo	Dam	236	L	5	5	0
3rd Lake Washington Floating Bridge I-90, Seattle	1985 1987	Washington DOT	Atkinson	Bridge Approach	36	CFL	10	10	0
First Hill Lid Structure, I-90 Mercer Is, WA	1987 1989	Washington DOT	Paschen Constructors	Roadways & Lid	66	AC	11	11	0
Seattle Lid, I-90 Seattle	1987 1990	Washington DOT	Kiewit-Atkinson	Roadways & Lid	65	A	2	2	0
Mt. St. Helens Highway Replacement Hoff. Crk - Geo. Ridge, WA	1988 1990	Washington DOT	Ledcor/Seacon	Replace SR 504	7	A	0	0	0
University Ave Reconstructed Sewer Honolulu	1988 1990	City & County of Honolulu	Coluccio	24" sewer	2	L	1	1	0
Seattle Transit Access Seattle	1988 1991	Washington DOT	Kiewit	I-5 to I-90 Interchange	54	A	0	0	0
Mt. St. Helens Highway Replacement Geo. Ridge to Elk Rock, WA	1989 1991	Washington DOT	West Co.	Replace SR 504	8	A	0	0	0
Mt. St. Helens Highway Replacement Hoffstadt section, WA	1989 1991	Washington DOT	Koney	Replace SR 504	13	A	0	0	0
Seattle Transit Access Seattle	1989 1991	Washington DOT	Kiewit	I-5 to I-90 Interchange	27	A	0	0	0
Mt. St. Helens Highway Replacement Hoffstadt Crk Bridge, WA	1989 1991	Washington DOT	Selby Br.	Replace SR 504	13	A	1	1	0
L. V. Morrow Bridge Renovation, I-90 Seattle, WA	1989 1992	Washington DOT	Traylor	Structure	36	A	1 (Issues Remain)	1	0
74th to Island Crest Way, I-90 Mercer Island, WA	1989 1992	Washington DOT	DBM	Roadways	31	A	1	1	0
First Hill Lid Eastbound, I-90 Mercer Island, WA	1989 1992	Washington DOT	Atkinson	Roadways and Lid	48	A	0	0	0

PROJECT NAME AND LOCATION	YEARS	OWNER	CONTRACTOR	DESCRIPTION	COST $ million	KEY	DISPUTES HEARD	SETTLED	LITIGATED
Hanging Lake Viaduct, Glenwood Springs, CO	1989 1993	Colorado DOT	Flatiron/Prescon JV	I-70	37	A	12	12	0
Harbor Freeway, I-110, Los Angeles	1989 1993	Cal Trans	C. C. Myers, Inc.	Diamond Lanes	81	LW	4	4	0
Century Freeway, I-105 @ I-91, Los Angeles	1989 1993	Cal Trans	C. C. Myers, Inc.	HOV Lanes	31	LW	2	2	0
1,500 Acre Subdivision, Burlingame, CA	1990 1992	Shea Homes	Granite	Grading & Drainage	20	A	Board never setup	0	0
Boston Harbor Outfall Diffuser Shafts, Boston, MA	1990 1992	MA Water Res Auth	Cashman, Interbeton	drilled shafts, 3 ft dia by 240 ft deep in Bay	77	D	0	0	0
Shoshone Dam I/C Bridge, Glenwood Springs, CO	1990 1992	Colorado DOT	Centric-Jones	I-70	23	A	1	1	0
Seattle Lid Eastbound, I-90, Seattle	1990 1992	Washington DOT	Kiewit	Roadways and Lid	39	A	0	0	0
23rd Avenue, I-90, Seattle	1990 1992	Washington DOT	Mowat	Roadways	26	A	Issues remain	0	0
Mt. St. Helens Highway Replacement, Elk Rock to Maratta Creek, WA	1990 1992	Washington DOT	Kiewit	Replace SR 504	25	A	1	1	0
Bellvue Transit Access, Ph 1, Seattle	1991 1992	Washington DOT	General Construction	I-90 Interchange	17	A	2	2	0
Mt. St. Helens Highway Replacement, Maratta Creek to Coldwater, WA	1991 1993	Washington DOT	Kiewit	Replace SR 504	10	A	0	0	0
Kalanianaole Highway, Ph 1, Honolulu	1991 1993	Hawaii DOT	Hawaiian Dredging	Roadways	37	A	2	2	0
Luther Burbank to N. Mercer, I-90, Mercer Island, WA	1992 1993	Washington DOT	Kuney	Roadways	29	A	0	0	0
Renton 'S' Curves, Utility Tunnels, I-405, Seattle	1992 1993	Washington DOT	Atkinson	Structure and short tunnels	34	A	3	3	0
Milner Hydro Electric Project, Twin Falls, ID	1992 1993	Idaho Power Company	Mortenson	Structure	15	L	1	1	0

PROJECT NAME AND LOCATION	YEARS	OWNER	CONTRACTOR	DESCRIPTION	COST $ million	KEY	DISPUTES HEARD	SETTLED	LITIGATED
L. V. Morrow Bridge Replacement I-90, Seattle, WA	1992 1993	Washington DOT	General, Rainier	Floating Bridge	74	A	0	0	0
TOTALS, COMPLETED HEAVY - HIGHWAY				31 EACH	$1.2 BILLION		72	72	0

BUILDING & PROCESS

PROJECT NAME AND LOCATION	YEARS	OWNER	CONTRACTOR	DESCRIPTION	COST $ million	KEY	DISPUTES HEARD	SETTLED	LITIGATED
Eisenhower Tunnel, 2nd Bore Loveland Pass, Colorado	1975 1977	Colorado DOT	Howard Electric	Electrical in Vent Buildings	7	A	13	13	0
Newsprint Mill Granada, MS	1986 1989	News South, Inc.	Rust Intl. and Natl. Ind. Constrs	Newsprint Mill	250	LO	0	0	0
America West Arena Phoenix, AZ	1990 1992	City of Phoenix	Mardian Const.	Phoenix Suns Basketball Arena	47	H	0 Board never met	0	0
Inter-Island Terminal Honolulu, HI	1990 1993	Hawaii DOT	Kiewit Pacific	Airport Terminal	131	A	2	2	0
Office Complex Alpharetta, GA	1991 1992	AT & T	HCB	Office Buildings	19	A	0	0	0
Convert Mfg to Office Orlando, FL	1992 1993	AT & T	Huber, Hunt & Nichols	Office Buildings	8	A	0	0	0
Philadelphia Convention Ctr. Philadelphia, PA	? ?		2 contracts		50	?			
TOTALS, COMPLETED BUILDING & PROCESS				8 EACH	$0.5 BILLION		15	15	0
TOTALS, COMPLETED CONTRACTS				68 EACH	$2.7 BILLION		124	123	0

CONTRACTS UNDER CONSTRUCTION

TUNNELS & UNDERGROUND

PROJECT NAME AND LOCATION	YEARS	OWNER	CONTRACTOR	TUNNEL LENGTH feet	DIAMETER feet	COST $ million	KEY	DISPUTES HEARD	SETTLED	LITIGATED
Cumberland Gap Tunnel Cumberland Gap, TN	1990 1993	FHWA for NPS	S. A. Healy, Lodigiani	two at 4,200	40	52	PT	15	95% complete 1	0 Dispute may be litigated
Boston Harbor Outfall Tunnel Boston, MA	1990 1994	Mass Water Res Auth	Kiewit, Atkinson, Kenny	49,500	25	202	D	6	40% complete 6	0 More disputes to hear

PROJECT NAME AND LOCATION	YEARS	OWNER	CONTRACTOR	DESCRIPTION		COST $ million	KEY	DISPUTES HEARD	SETTLED	LITIGATED
Crystal Springs Water Project Half Moon Bay, CA	1991 1994	Coastside Water Dist	J. H. Pomeroy	600 + 15,000 ft pipeline	7	6	A	95% complete	1	0
Metro Red Line, B221 Vermont-Western Line + Sta, LA	1991 1994	Los Angeles Transit Comm	Tutor-Saliba, Perini	two at 4,800	19	80	?	99% complete	0	0
H-3 Halawa Tunnels Honolulu	1991 1994	Hawaii DOT	Hawaiian Dredge & Ohbayashi	two at 1,800	45	89	A	95% complete	0	0
Metro Red Line, B231 Wilshire/Western Station, LA	1991 1994	Los Angeles Transit Comm	Tutor-Saliba & Perini	Cut & Cover Transit Station		54	?	90% complete	0	0
NC-1B Tunnels and Undg Station Dallas	1991 1994	Dallas Area Rapid Tran.	S. A. Healy	11,000	20	94	A	75% complete	0	0
Metro Red Line, B201 Alvarado to Vermont Line, LA	1991 1994	Los Angeles Transit Comm	Tutor-Saliba, Perini	two at 3,405	19	45	?	90% complete	0	0
Metro Red Line, B211 Wilshire/Vermont Station, LA	1991 1994	Los Angeles Transit Comm	Tutor-Saliba & Perini	Cut & Cover Transit Station		45	?	70% complete	0	0
Inter-Island Tunnel Boston, MA	1991 1994	MA Water Res Auth	S. A. Healy, Modern Cont.	25,000	11	73	D	50% complete More disputes to hear	21	16
Lesotho Highlands Transfer Tunnel Lesotho, Africa	1991 1997	Leshoto High Dev. Auth	LHPC	145,000	16	460	L	50% complete Disputes to hear	0	0
Immersed Tube, I-90, Central Artery Boston, MA	1992 1995	Mass DOT	M-K, Interbeton, J. F. White	4,000		227	DM	50% complete	1	1
Metro Red Line, B251 Vermont to Hollywood Line, LA	1993 1996	Los Angeles Co Transit Comm	Shea, Kiewit, Kenny	two at 31,600	19	172	D	20% complete 3 Disputes to hear		
Ertan Project, Sichuan Prov. Peoples Republic of China	1992 1998	Ertan Hydro Development	Philip Holzman & JV Partners	3,300 Megawatt Undg Powerhouse		444	A	20% complete	0	0
Pleasant Hill Interceptor Martinez, CA	1993 1994	Cent Contra Costa Sanitary Dist.	Ranger Pipeline Company	2,000 + 17,000 ft pipeline	9	14	A	Board being organized		
Soft ground tunnel Ft. Knox, KY	1993 1994	COE	W. L. Hailey			6	H	DRB never met	0	0
14th Avenue Interceptor, IA Kenosha, WI	1993 1995	City of Kenosha	Super Excavators	6,000	8	9	A	90% complete	0	0

PROJECT NAME AND LOCATION	YEARS	OWNER	CONTRACTOR	DESCRIPTION		COST $ million	KEY	STATUS / DISPUTES	HEARD	SETTLED	LITIGATED
Lower 'K' Development San Manual, AZ	1993 1995	Magma Copper Co.	Frontier-Kemper	33,200	15	33	AP	5% complete			
14th Avenue Interceptor, IB Kenosha, WI	1993 1995	City of Kenosha	Michael's Pipeleine	7,000 jacked pipe	7	5	A	Board never organized			0
St. Clair River Tunnel Port Huron, MI	1993 1996	CN North America	Traylor & Asso	6,050	27	53	AP	20% complete	0	0	0
West Hills Tunnel Portland, OR	1993 1996	Tri-Met	Frontier-Kemper + Traylor	two at 16,000	19	104	A	10% complete	0	0	0
Richmond Transport Fac. San Francisco, CA	1993 1996	City of San Francisco	Shank, Balfour Beatty	11,100	14	30	A	5% complete	0	0	0
B-11A Washington, D.C.	1993 1996	WMATA	J. F. Shea	two at 5,400	17	50	LMN	Board being organized			
Sewer Contract E San Francisco, CA	1993 1996	City of San Francisco	Kajima	1,150	10	20	A	Board being organized			
San Francisco Muni-Turnaround San Francisco, CA	1993 1997	City of San Francisco	Tutor-Saliba-Perini	1,700	16	95	A	Board appointed			
Metro Red Line, C331 Universal City to No Holly., LA	1993 1996	Los Angeles Co Transit Comm	Obayashi	two at 10,500	19	65	D	Board being organized			
Metro Red Line, B241 Vermont/Beverly Station, LA	1993 1997	Los Angeles Co Transit Comm	Tutor-Saliba-Perini	Cut & Cover Transit Station		41	D	Board being organized			
Metro Red Line, B252 Vermont/Santa Mon. Sta., LA	1993 1997	Los Angeles Co Transit Comm	Kiewit-Shea	Cut & Cover Transit Station		51	D	Board being organized			
Metro Red Line, B261 Vermont/Sunset Station, LA	1993 1997	Los Angeles Co Transit Comm	Tutor-Saliba-Perini	Cut & Cover Transit Station		45	D	Awaiting award			
Metro Red Line, B271 Hollywood/Western Sta, LA	1993 1997	Los Angeles Co Transit Comm	PCL	Cut & Cover Transit Station		37	D	Awarded			
Metro Red Line, B281 Hollywood/Vine Station, LA	1993 1997	Los Angeles Co Transit Comm	Kajima-Wilson	Cut & Cover Transit Station		49	D	Awarded			
Nathpa Jhakri Project Northwest India	1993 1998	Nathpa Jhakri Power Corp.	Impregilo + 3 other contractors	Dam, tunnels and Underground Powerhouse		100	A	Awarded			
TOTALS, TUNNELS & UNDG UNDER CONSTRUCTION				34 EACH		$2.9 BILLION			30	24	0

96

HEAVY - HIGHWAY

PROJECT NAME AND LOCATION	YEARS	OWNER	CONTRACTOR	DESCRIPTION	COST $ million	KEY	DISPUTES HEARD	SETTLED	LITIGATED
Century Freeway, Los Angeles	1989 1994	Cal Trans	Kasler	I-105 to I-405 Interchange	124	LW	95% complete, 2	2	0
H-3 Windward Viaduct, Honolulu	1990 1993	Hawaii DOT	SCI/Black	Long Span Segmental Viaduct	136	AF	99% complete, 42 / 9 disputes to hear	38	0
Century Freeway, Los Angeles	1990 1993	Cal Trans	MCM Construction	I-105 to I-710 Interchange	80	LW	90% complete, 5	4	0
Century Freeway, Los Angeles	1990 1993	Cal Trans	Ball, Ball & Brosamer	Roadways & Haz Waste Removal	53	LW	85% complete, 4	3	0
Haliewa Bypass, Honolulu, HI	1991 1993	Hawaii DOT	Fletcher-Pacific	Structures	23	A	98% complete, 1	0	0
Mill Seat Landfill, Monroe County, NY	1991 1993	Monroe County	H. E. Sargent	Sanitary Landfill	29	A	90% complete, 0 / 1 dispute to hear	0	0
Natchez Trace Pkwy Bridge, Nashville, TN	1991 1994	FHWA	PCL Constrs	Precast Segmental Concrete Arch Br	14	T	30% complete, 0	0	0
Cowlitz Falls Project, Morton, WA	1991 1995	Lewis Co. PUD District #1	Torno-America	Hydro Project	55	A	95% complete, 3 / More disputes to hear	3	0
Katse Dam, Lesotho Highlands Proj, Lesotho, Africa	1991 1997	Leshoto High Dev. Auth	Impregilo JV	250 MCY dam	320	L	35% complete, 0	0	0
Snohomish River Bridge, SR 2, Everett, WA	1992 1993	Washington DOT	Atkinson	Structure	19	A	99% complete, 1	1	0
405/NE 8th St Interchange, SR 405, Bellevue, WA	1992 1993	Washington DOT	Kiewit	Structure	28	A	70% complete, 2	2	0
Coal Creek to N.E. 8th, SR 405, Bellevue, WA	1992 1993	Washington DOT	Leadcore	Roadway	12	A	85% complete, 0	0	0
Pittsburg-Antioch Extension, Contra Costa Co, CA	1992 1994	Bay Area RTD San Francisco	Tutor-Saliba	Line Section, Concord-No Concord	48	D	40% complete, 0	0	0
OC-2 Section, Dallas, TX	1992 1994	Dallas Area Rapid Transit	Hensel-Phelps	5,000 foot bridge + 5,000 feet at grade	19	A	80% complete, 0	0	0

PROJECT NAME AND LOCATION	YEARS	OWNER	CONTRACTOR	DESCRIPTION	COST $ million	KEY	DISPUTES HEARD	SETTLED	LITIGATED
Twin S Curve Renton, WA	1992 1994	Washington DOT	Atkinson	Widen & Realign	35	A	70% complete	0	0
C & O Canal Bridge Wilmington, DE	1992 1995	Deleware DOT	Recchi America	Concrete Segmental Cable Stayed Bridge	74	A	25% complete	0	0
H-3 North Halava Valley Viaduct Honolulu	1992 1995	Hawaii DOT	Kiewit	Long Span Segmental Viaduct	141	A	50 % complete	0	0
Ertan Project, Sichuan Prov. Peoples Republic of China	1992 1998	Ertan Hydro Development	Impregilo & JV Partners	3,300 Megawatt Dam & Appurtances	625	A	33% complete	0	0
Twin Falls Project Twin Falls, ID	1993 1994	Idaho Power Company	TIC	Addition to Hydro Electric Plant	8	A	20% complete	0	0
Kalanianaole Highway, Ph 2 Honolulu	1993 1994	Hawaii DOT	Kiewit	Roadways	35	A	30% complete	0	0
NC-1A Transition - tunnel to surface Dallas	1993 1994	Dallas Area Rapid Transit	Rosiek Const.	Cut & cover	10	A	60% complete	2	2
Jones Rd to Maplewood Seattle	1993 1994	Washington DOT	Kiewit	Roadway	12	A	30% complete	0	0
Green River Interchange Seattle	1993 1994	Washington DOT	PCI	Roadway	7	A	35% complete	0	0
Snohomish River Bridge, P2 Everett	1993 1994	Washington DOT	General Const.	Structures	10	A	60% complete	0	0
Bellvue Transit Access, Ph 2 Seattle	1993 1995	Washington DOT	Max J. Kuney	I-90 Interchange	18	A	55% complete	0	0
H-3 Project Honolulu	1993 1995	Hawaii DOT	Kiewit Pacific	Mech-Elect & Tunnel Finish	31	A	30% complete	0	0
OC-1 Dallas	1993 1995	Dallas Area Rapid Transit	Neosho	9,500 feet at grade wit Amtrack interfaces	15	A	60% complete	0	0
Northrup to Bothel, SR 405 Bellvue, WA	1993 1995	Washington DOT	Max J. Kuney	Roadway	25	A	50% complete	0	0
No Halawa Valley Hwy, Unit 1, Ph 1A Honolulu	1993 1995	Hawaii DOT	Hawaiian Dredging	Roadway Reconstruction	25	A	5% complete	0	0
Mt. St. Helens Highway Repl. Coldwater to Johnson, WA	1993 1995	Washington DOT	Washington Constructors	Replace SR 504	25	A	60% complete	0	0

PROJECT NAME AND LOCATION	YEARS	OWNER	CONTRACTOR	DESCRIPTION	COST $ million	KEY	DISPUTES HEARD	SETTLED	LITIGATED
Pittsburg-Antioch Extension Contra Costa Co, CA	1993 1995	Bay Area RTD San Francisco	Conco Cement Company	North Concord/ Martinez Sta	24	D	10% complete	0	0
Colma Station Extension, 12YC-110 San Mateo Co, CA	1993 1995	Bay Area RTD San Francisco	Dillingham	Station, Line & TRackwork	42	D	5% complete	0	0
Three Projects Bangladesh	1993 1995	World Bank		Bridges & River Bank Protection	100	?	10% complete	0	0
Colma Station Extension, 12YS-110 San Matro Co, CA	1993 1995	Bay Area RTD San Francisco	Morse Diesel/ Bomel	Parking Str & Bridges	25	D	0% complete	0	0
Dublin-Pleasanton Extn, 08ys-110 Alameda Co, CA	1993 1995	Bay Area RTD San Francisco	Walsh-Pacific	Castro Valley Sta & Parking	18	D	0% complete	0	0
195th to 164th SW HOV, Stage 2 Seattle	1993 1995	Washington DOT	Max J. Kuney	Roadway	30	A	5% complete	0	0
Central Business District, at-grade Dallas, TX	1993 1996	Dallas Area Rapid Transit	Gilbert-Texas	7,000 feet light rail and three stations	44	A	5% complete	0	0
New Haven to Boston Conn. and Mass.	1993 1997	Amtrack	MK-Comstock-Spie	Upgrade rail	350	?	Construction start 1994	0	0
Evergreen Point Bridge Seattle	1994 1995	Washington DOT	Atkinson	Structure Rehabilitation	17	A	0% complete	0	0
Snohomish - Ebey Bridge, Stage 2 Seattle	1994 1996	Washington DOT	General Const.	Structures	10	A	5% complete	0	0
Seven Oaks Dam San Bernadino, CA	1994 1997	COE	??? bid protest	38 million CY earthfill dam	180	AP	Awaiting award		
TOTALS, HEAVY - HIGHWAY UNDER CONSTRUCTION				43 EACH	$2.9 BILLION		62	55	0

BUILDING & PROCESS

City Hall Phoenix, AZ	1991 1994	City of Phoenix	Huber, Hunt & Nichols	20 story, 450,000 SF	45	H	95% complete	0	0
Akron Convention Center Akron, Ohio	1992 1994	City of Akron, Ohio	CM = Ruhlin Co. 19 Genl Contrs	Convention Center	24	A	70% complete	1	1
Twin Towers Correctional Facility Los Angeles	1991 1994	Los Angeles County	Newberg/Dick	Jail, hospital & central plant	373	A	93% complete	3	2
Lynwood Regional Justice Center	1991	Los Angeles	Newberg	Jail, court	194	A	98% complete		

99

PROJECT NAME AND LOCATION	YEARS	OWNER	CONTRACTOR	DESCRIPTION	COST $ million	KEY	DISPUTES HEARD	SETTLED	LITIGATED
Lynwood, CA	1994	County		& sheriff station			7	6	0
Health Science Building Seattle	1991 1994	Univ of Washington	SDL Corp	New Educational Building	33	A	90% complete 0	0	0
Physics & Astronomy Bldg Seattle	1991 1994	Univ of Washington	Mortenson Construction	New Educational Building	46	A	90 % complete 0	0	0
H-3 Project Honolulu	1991 1995	Hawaii DOT	TLT Babcock	Vent Fans & Acc	19	A	80% complete 0	0	0
Chemistry Science Building Seattle	1992 1994	Univ of Washington	Ellis-Don Construction	New Educational Building	27	A	90 % completee 0	0	0
Biomedical Science Building Seattle	1992 1994	Univ of Washington	Ellis-Don Construction	New Educational Building	40	A	90 % complete 0	0	0
H-3 Project Honolulu	1992 1995	Hawaii DOT	JPW Controls	Control Systems	20	A	30% complete 0	0	0
Comprehensive High School Everett, WA	1993 1994	Everett School Dist.	Mortenson Construction	New Educational Building	24	A	80 % complete 0	0	0
Wastewater Treatment Plant Martinez, CA	1993 1994	Cent Contra Costa Sanitary District	Humphry Construction	Headwork	18	A	60 % complete 0	0	0
Phoenix Central Library Phoenix, AZ	1993 1995	City of Phoenix	Sundt Corp	Library	27	H	30% complete 0	0	0
Secondary Treatment Plant Fresno, CA	1993 1996	City of Fresno	Western Summit Constructors	Upgrade Plant	82	A	Board being organized		
Makai Expansion, Inter-Island Airport Terminal, Honolulu	1994 1995	Hawaii DOT	Hawaiian Dredging	Add five gates to new terminal	19	AP	Awaiting award		
Prisons Texas	1994 1996	TX Dept of Criminal Justice	5 contracts		165	H			
Phase III Headquarter Expansion Washington, D.C.	1994 1996	International Monetary Fund	Heery/Donohoe	Commercial Office Bldg	80	?	Awarded, Await Notice to Proceed		
TOTALS, BUILDING & PROCESS UNDER CONSTRUCTION				21 EACH	$1.2 BILLION		11	9	0
TOTALS, CONTRACTS UNDER CONSTRUCTION				98 EACH	$7.0 BILLION		103	88	0
TOTALS, CONTRACTS COMPLETED & UNDER CONSTRUCTION				166 EACH	$9.7 BILLION		227	211	0

CONTRACTS PLANNED

TUNNELS & UNDERGROUND

PROJECT NAME AND LOCATION	YEARS	OWNER	CONTRACTOR	DESCRIPTION	TUNNEL LENGTH feet	DIAMETER feet	COST $ million	KEY	DISPUTES HEARD SETTLED LITIGATED
Dwamish River/1st Ave. South Seattle	1994 1995	City of Seattle		Utility relocation	500	10	7	A	bids 1994
Metro Red Line, C411 Wil/West to Pico/SanVin., LA	1994 1996	Los Angeles Co Transit Comm		two at 10,000		19	120	D	bids 1994 ???
Lexington North Rochester, NY	1994 1996	Monroe County		4,700		10	7		Bids 1994 ???
Metro Red Line, C311 Sta 630 to Univ City, LA	1994 1997	Los Angeles Co Transit Comm		two at 13,370		19	180	D	bids 1994
Provo Canyon Tunnels Provo, UT	1994 1997	Utah DOT		three at 400		29	20		bids 1994
Metro Red Line, C301 Holly-Highland Station, LA	1994 1997	Los Angeles Co Transit Comm		Cut & Cover Transit Station			80	D	Bids 1994
Mt Hope - Rosedale Rochester, NY	1994 1997	Monroe County		8,100		12	14		Bids 1994 ???
Senaca-Norton, Phase 2 Rochester, NY	1994 1997	Monroe County		6,500		12	11		Bids 1994 ???
Glenmont Storage Yard Washington, DC	1994 1996	WMATA		Grading, drainage & trackwork			20	MN	Bids 1994
Glenmont Station Washington, DC	1994 1997	WMATA		Cut & cover			36	MN	Bids 1994
Mid-City Route, E-2C Washington, D.C.	1994 1997	WMATA		two at 3,100		18	45	MN	Bids 1994
Mid-City Route, E-4A Washington, D.C.	1994 1997	WMATA		Cut & Cover Transit Station			60	MN	Bids 1994
Mid-City Route, E-4B Washington, D.C.	1994 1997	WMATA		two at 6,700		18	85	MN	Bids 1994
Mid-City Route, E-3A Washington, D.C.	1994 1997	WMATA		Cut & Cover Transit Station			65	MN	Bids 1994

PROJECT NAME AND LOCATION	YEARS	OWNER	CONTRACTOR	DESCRIPTION		COST $ million	KEY	DISPUTES HEARD SETTLED LITIGATED
Mid-City Route, E-3B Washington, D.C.	1994 1997	WMATA		two at 3,200	18	40	MN	Bids 1994
Metro Red Line, C351 North Hollywood Station, LA	1994 1998	Los Angeles Co Transit Comm		Cut & Cover Station & Crossover		70	D	Bids 1994
Effluent/Storage Tunnel Atlanta, GA	1994 1998	City of Atlanta		41,000	26	110		Bids 1994
Metro Red Line, C321 Universal City Station, LA	1994 1998	Los Angeles Co Transit Comm		Cut & Cover Station & Crossover		75	D	Bids 1994
West Seattle Tunnel Seattle	1994 1998	Seattle Metro		10,500	9	25	A	Bids 1994
Metro Red Line, C421 Pico/San Vincente Sta, LA	1994 1998	Los Angeles Co Transit Comm		Cut & Cover Transit Station		120	D	Bids 1994 ???
Central Artery Project Boston, MA	1994 1998	Mass DOT	6 contracts	Cut & Cover Freeway		1309	DJTZ	Bid 1994 - 1996
Transit Expansion Projects Toronto, Ontario	1994 1999	Toronto Transit Commission	32 contracts	Tunnels, C&C Stations, Surface & Other		1440	A	Bid 1994 - 1996
Metro Red Line, C401 Crenshaw/Olympic Station, LA	1995 1998	Los Angeles Co Transit Comm		Cut & Cover Transit Station		100	D	Bids 1995 ???
Point Loma Tunnel San Diego, CA	1995 1998	Clean Water Program Greater San Diego		55,000	12	160	A	Bids 1995
River Mountain Pumped Storage Proj. Arkansas	1995 2000	Consol Pumped Storage, Inc.		Underground Powerhouse & Tunnels		350	A	Bids 1995
Outer "F" Line, F-6 A Washington, DC	1996 1999	WMATA		2 @ 4,00 + Cut & Cover Station	18	100	D	Bids 1996
Elk Creek Tunnel Drain, OR	1997 1999	Oregon DOT		1,200	40	20	A	bids 1996
TOTALS, TUNNELS PLANNED				63 EACH		4.7 BILLION		

HEAVY - HIGHWAY

PROJECT NAME AND LOCATION	YEARS	OWNER	CONTRACTOR	DESCRIPTION	COST $ million	KEY	DISPUTES HEARD SETTLED LITIGATED
Snohomish - Ebey Bridge, Stage 3 Seattle	1994 1995	Washington DOT		Structures	19	A	Bids 1994
No Halawa Valley Hwy, Unit 2	1994	Hawaii		Structures	47	A	Bids 1994

PROJECT NAME AND LOCATION	YEARS	OWNER	CONTRACTOR	DESCRIPTION	COST $ million	KEY	DISPUTES HEARD SETTLED / LITIGATED
Honolulu	1995	DOT					
Black Diamond - SE 312th, Stage 1 Seattle	1994 1995	Washington DOT		Raodway	29	A	Bids 1994
Duwamish River/First Ave Soutn Br. Seattle	1994 1996	Washington DOT		Bridge	80	A	Bids 1994
No Halawa Valley Hwy, Unit 1, Ph 1B Honolulu	1994 1995	Hawaii DOT		Structures	20	A	Bids 1994
Tukwila to Lucille St., Stage 1 Seattle	1994 1996	Washington DOT		Raodway & Structure Widening	29	A	Bids 1994
Various Highway Projects California	1994 1996	Cal Trans	40 contracts		1000	W	Bids 1994
SR 18, Issaquah - Hobart I/C+ Raging River Bridge, Seattle	1994 1996	Washington DOT		Interchange	22	A	Bids 1994
NC-2 Dallas	1994 1996	Dallas Area Rapid Transit		13,000 feet at grade + 3 stations	20	A	Bids May 1994
Issaquah-Hobart & Bridge Seattle	1994 1996	Washington DOT		Raodway & Structures	22	A	Bids 1994
Pierce to Tukwila HOV, Climbing Lane Seattle	1994 1996	Washington DOT		Raodway Widening	21	A	Bids 1994
Tukwila to Lucille St., Stage 2 Seattle	1994 1997	Washington DOT		Raodway & Structure Widening	35	A	Bids 1994
Central Artery Project Boston, MA	1994 1998	Mass DOT	8 contracts	Raodway & Structures	553	DJTZ	Bid 1994 - 1996
Portland Bridge Replacement Project Portland, ME	1994 1998	Maine Dept of Transportation	5 contracts	Bascule Bridge	150	A	Bid 1994
Tukwila to Lucille St., Stage 3 Seattle	1995 1997	Washington DOT		Raodway & Structure Widening	30	A	Bids 1995
SR-167, Auburn to Kent HOV Seattle	1995 1997	Washington DOT		Raodway	30	A	Bids 1995 ???
SR 405, Tukwila to Factoria Seattle	1995 1997	Washington DOT		Raodway	25	A	Bids 1995
Duwamsih - 1st Ave Bridge Rehab	1995	Washington		Rehab	42	A	Bids 1995

PROJECT NAME AND LOCATION	YEARS	OWNER	CONTRACTOR	DESCRIPTION	COST $ million	KEY	DISPUTES HEARD / SETTLED / LITIGATED
Seattle	1998	DOT					
Metro Red Line, C401 Crenshaw/Olympic Station, LA	1995 1998	Los Angeles Co Transit Comm		Cut & Cover Station	60	D	Bids 1995
Offshore Riser & Outfall Connection San Diego, CA	1996 1997	Clean Water Program Greater San Diego			20		Bids 1996
SE 312th Way - SE 304th St Seattle	1996 1997	Washington DOT		Raodway Widening	29	A	Bids 1996
Longtan Project, Guanxi Prov. Peoples Republic of China	1995 2002	Longtan Hydro Development			1000		Bids 1995
Outer "F" Line, F-6 B Washington, DC	1996 1999	WMATA		Retained cut Station + line	100	MN	Bids 1996
Outer "F" Line, F-7 Washington, DC	1996 1999	WMATA		Aerial line + Station	90	MN	Bids 1996
Outer "F" Line, F-9 Washington, DC	1996 1999	WMATA		Station & Line at Grad	80	MN	Bids 1996
Outer "F" Line, F-10 Washington, DC	1996 1999	WMATA		Station & Line at Grad	80	MN	Bids 1996

TOTALS, HEAVY - HIGHWAY PLANNED 76 EACH 3.6 BILLION

BUILDING & PROCESS

PROJECT NAME AND LOCATION	YEARS	OWNER	CONTRACTOR	DESCRIPTION	COST $ million	KEY	DISPUTES HEARD / SETTLED / LITIGATED
Art Museum Phoenix, AZ	1994 1996	City of Phoenix		Renovation & Restoration	18	H	bids too high may be rebid
Inter Island Terminal, Phase II Honolulu	1994 1996	Hawaii DOT		Airport Terminal	19	A	Bids 5-94
Parking Structure Akron, OH	1994 1995	City of Akron		7 story, 700 car deck Will use same DRB as Convention Center	9	U	Bids 3-94
Central Artery Project Boston, MA	1994 1998	Mass DOT	4 contracts	Process & Control Buildings	200	DJTZ	Bid 1994 - 1996
Prisons Texas	1994 1996	Texas Dept of Criminal Justice	25 contracts	Prisons	590	H	Bid 1994 & 1995
Pt Loma Water Treat Plant Tie-In	1995	Clean Water Program			15		Bids 1995

PROJECT NAME AND LOCATION	YEARS	OWNER	CONTRACTOR	DESCRIPTION	COST $ million	KEY	DISPUTES HEARD SETTLED LITIGATED
San Diego, CA	1998	Greater San Diego					
TOTALS, BUILDING & PROCESS PLANNED				33 EACH	0.9 BILLION		
TOTALS, CONTRACTS PLANNED				172 EACH	$9.2 BILLION		
TOTALS, ALL PROJECTS				338 EACH	$18.9 BILLION		

KEYS

A   ASCE DRB specification, current at time of construction, used without variation, or conformed to all critical provisions of that ASCE specification.

The following keys show variations of the ASCE DRB specification and other features of contracts.

B   Binding recommendations by Board, rather than non-binding as provided by ASCE specification.

C   Major claims settled without referral to the Board.

D   Delayed access to Board via General Conditions Disputes provision requiring submittal and review before DRB hearing.

F   Problems in design resulted in many disputes.

H   Board heard disputes only; Board did not attend progress meetings or receive progress reports.

J   Jurisdiction of Board was limited to large disputes.

L   Late. Board was established after disputes arose.

M   Members selected by each Party nominating three members and then selecting one member from other Parties list.
    First two members selected Chair. Parties did not approve members.

N   Owner and Contractor personnel observed Board deliberations.

O   One person functioned as DRB.

P   Partnering was included in contract.

R   Recommendations were not admissible in subsequent settlement proceedings.

S   Owner could refuse to take a dispute to the Board.

T   Jurisdiction of Board was limited to technical issues.

U   Included provisions for Board to hear Sub-contractor disputes.

V   Low maximum limit was placed on billing rate of Board members.

W   Some of the members were not neutral.

X   Either party could require appointment of a new Board for future disputes.

Y   Optional. Either party could request establishment of the Board.

Z   Board members were required to indemnify Owner and Contractor.

Appendix **B**

Case Histories

Introduction

The experience of owners and contractors on completed projects employing DRBs is indicative of the merit of this process. The following case histories describe completed DRB projects for each category of construction. They provide sources for anyone considering a DRB to verify its value on past works.

Case histories were chosen according to the following criteria:

1. Historical significance to the DRB process
2. Unusual project
3. Interesting DRB or dispute experience
4. Geographic diversity
5. Broad range of contract cost
6. Completed project with all disputes settled
7. Not presented in previous editions of this manual

The following industry abbreviations have been used:

CM	construction manager
DOT	Department of Transportation
HOV	high occupancy vehicle
JV	joint venture
NTP	notice to proceed
SF	square foot
SR	state route
TPA	three-party agreement

Case	Location	Disputes
Tunnels and Underground		
1. Bradley Lake	Alaska	0
2. Lehigh Tunnel	Pennsylvania	0
3. San Antonio	Texas	13
Heavy Highway		
4. Bellevue Transit Access	Seattle	2
5. Hanging Lake Viaduct	Colorado	12
6. Lacey V. Murrow Bridge	Seattle	0
7. Sr 405 Interchange	Seattle	2
Building and Process		
8. America West Arena	Phoenix	0
9. Inter-Island Airport	Honolulu	2
10. Office Building Complex	Atlanta	0
11. Convention Center	Akron	1

Case History 1

PROJECT: BRADLEY LAKE HYDROELECTRIC PROJECT, Homer, AK, GENERAL CIVIL CONTRACT

DESCRIPTION: 125 foot high by 610 foot long concrete-faced rockfill dam, diversion tunnel completion, excavation and lining of 18,600 foot by 13 foot diameter power tunnel, 720 foot power shaft, gate shaft, penstock bifurcations, and excavation for surface powerhouse.

CONSTRUCTED: 1988–1991

PROVISIONS: 1989 ASCE DRB specification modified to require the Contractor to submit a fully documented and quantified claim to the construction manager. Contractor may appeal CM finding to DRB.

RECORD: Disputes Heard: 0

Disputes Litigated: 0

COSTS: Estimate: $118 million

Bid: $91 million

Final: $89 million

OWNER:	Alaska Energy Authority, Anchorage
DESIGNER:	Stone & Webster Engineering Corp., Denver, CO
CM:	Bechtel Civil, San Francisco, CA
CONTRACTOR:	Ensearch Constructors, JV
DRB COST:	$140,000; 0.16% of final cost
REFERENCES:	Owner: Dave Eberle, Anchorage, AK
	CM: Harvey Elwin, San Francisco, CA
	Contractor: Jay Carlson, Chicago, IL
	DRB: Norman Nadel, Brewster, NY
REMARKS:	There were many disagreements; except for two, they were routinely settled. Disputes involving water inflows and welding of the steel tunnel liners, totaling over $8 million, were settled without going to the DRB.
	The owner's manager stated, "Although the DRB was never called upon to hear a dispute, I believe they were instrumental in the successful resolution of claims. The DRB was a catalyst which helped both the owner and the contractor to more objectively assess their relative positions. It also fostered an attitude of `let's resolve our differences in the field'!"

Case History 2

PROJECT:	LEHIGH TUNNEL #2, Lehigh & Carbon Counties, PA
DESCRIPTION:	32 foot diameter by 4500 foot long tunnel, a two-lane highway tunnel built using the New Austrian Tunneling Method (NATM). It is parallel to an existing tunnel built in 1957. Included grading, drainage, and paving of over a mile of approach roadways and maintenance of traffic. Portal structures, mechanical and electrical, by separate contracts.
CONSTRUCTED:	1989–1991
PROVISIONS:	1989 ASCE DRB specification added in Addendum 2

RECORD: Disputes Heard: 0
                       Disputes Litigated: 0
COSTS: Estimate: $43 million
                       Bid: $38 million
                       Final: $39 million
OWNER: Pennsylvania Turnpike Commission
DESIGNER: GSGSB/McCormick, Taylor & Associates, Inc.,
                       with Dr. G. Sauer Corp.
MANAGER: GSGSB/McCormick, Taylor & Associates, Inc.,
                       with Dr. G. Sauer Corp.
CONTRACTOR: Newberg-Walker-Rogers
DRB COST: $78,800; 0.20% of final cost
REFERENCES: Owner: Paul A. Edmunds, Harrisburg, PA
                       CM: Kenneth Pukita, Clark Summit, PA
                       Contractor: David E. Craven, Chicago, IL
                       DRB: Robert M. Matyas, Ithaca, NY
REMARKS: First bids were thrown out because of arith-
                       metic mistakes by the low bidder, who bid $33
                       million. No claims were submitted until after
                       the work was completed when a claim for $17
                       million was referred to the DRB. The parties
                       settled the claim prior to a hearing scheduled
                       by the board.

Case History 3

PROJECT: SAN ANTONIO RIVER AND SAN PEDRO
                       CREEK TUNNELS, PHASE II, San Antonio,
                       TX
DESCRIPTION: Two 25-foot lined diameter siphon tunnels
                       with inlet, outlet, maintenance, ventilation,
                       and instrumentation shafts (each about 140
                       feet deep).
                       San Antonio River Tunnel: 16,000 feet, 9 shafts
                       San Pedro Creek Tunnel: 5900 feet, 7 shafts
CONSTRUCTED: 1987–1993

PROVISIONS:	1989 ASCE DRB specification modified for the owner to require the contractor to submit a fully documented and quantified claim to the owner before going to DRB. Agreement of both parties required prior to appeal dispute to DRB.
RECORD:	Disputes Heard: 13
	Recommendations Accepted: 13
	Disputes Litigated: 0
COSTS:	Estimate: $53 million
	Bid: $48 million
	Final: $71 million
OWNER:	San Antonio River Authority/City of San Antonio
DESIGNER:	Parsons Brinckerhoff, Chicago, IL
CM:	Corps of Engineers, Ft. Worth District, TX
CONTRACTOR:	Obayashi Corporation
DRB COST:	$135,000; 0.19% of final cost
REFERENCES:	CM: Keith M. Allen, San Antonio, TX
	Contractor: Paul Zick, Boston, MA
	DRB: Robert J. Smith, Esq., Madison, WI
REMARKS:	The project initially experienced problems with erection tolerances and damage of the precast concrete segment final lining, and encountered unanticipated ground conditions. DRB first met 9 months after NTP. Two disputes concerned interpretation of the front documents, seven involved interpretations of the technical specifications, and four were changed conditions. Two recommendations were appealed back to the DRB for reconsideration.

Case History 4

PROJECT:	SR-90 BELLEVUE TRANSIT ACCESS and HOV LANES, Bellevue, WA

DESCRIPTION: Construction of an 1100 foot long HOV over-
pass through an extremely sensitive environ-
mental area. The project included the construction and widening of other bridges, retaining
walls, mitigation ponds, major utility reloca-
tions, and so on.

CONSTRUCTED: 1991–1992

PROVISIONS: Generally followed 1989 ASCE DRB specification. Included partnering.

RECORD: Disputes Heard: 2

Recommendations Accepted: 2

Disputes Litigated: 0

COSTS: Estimate: $15 million

Bid: $17 million

Final: $19 million

OWNER: Washington State Department of
Transportation

DESIGNER: Washington State Department of
Transportation

CONTRACTOR: General Construction & 3A Industries, JV

DRB COST: $50,000; 4 DRB meetings, 0.26% of final cost

REFERENCES: Owner: Phil Fordyce, Seattle,WA

Contractor: Robert McClure,

DRB: Raymond J. Dodson, Woodside, CA

REMARKS: The project had several unique milestones and
restraints, which included construction restric-
tions during a fish window, limited construction during Kingdome activities and
University of Washington football games, and
erection of structural steel over Highway I-90.
The project partnering agreement was instrumental in resolving several disputed issues .

Case History 5

PROJECT: HANGING LAKE VIADUCT, Glenwood
Canyon, CO

DESCRIPTION: Construction of two bridges on Highway I-70. Total length 8428 feet. Consisted of 34 feet wide by 10 feet deep precast concrete segments erected by balanced cantilever from the top using an overhead launching truss.

CONSTRUCTED: 1989–1993

PROVISIONS: Generally followed 1989 ASCE DRB specification.

RECORD: Disputes Heard: 12

Recommendations Accepted: 12

Disputes Litigated: 0

COSTS: Estimate: $40 million

Bid: $34 million

Final: $39 million

OWNER: Colorado DOT

DESIGNER: Figg Engineering

CONTRACTOR: Flatiron /Prescon Corp., JV

DRB COST: $50,000; 9 DRB meetings, 0.13% of final cost

REFERENCES: Owner: Glenn Violette, Glenwood Springs, CO

Contractor: Ray Schmahl, Longmont, CO

DRB: Raymond J. Dodson, Woodside, CA

REMARKS: An extremely complicated project executed in very limited work area over the Colorado River while maintaining traffic on the existing two-lane highway on one side of the canyon and a mainline railroad on the other side. Coordination was required with contractors on adjacent projects.

Case History 6

PROJECT: LACEY V. MURROW BRIDGE REPLACEMENT, Seattle, WA

DESCRIPTION: Replacement of 6600 feet of floating bridge consisting of 18 concrete pontoons, each approximately 360 feet long by 60 feet wide by 20 feet deep with two anchors each, and 2 pontoons 160 feet long by 60 feet wide by 20 feet deep with four anchors each.

CONSTRUCTED:	1992–1993
PROVISIONS:	Generally followed 1989 ASCE DRB specification. Included partnering.
RECORD:	Disputes Heard: 0
	Disputes Litigated: 0
COSTS:	Estimate: $86 million
	Bid: $74 million
	Final: $87 million
OWNER:	Washington State Department of Transportation
DESIGNER:	Washington State Department of Transportation
CONTRACTOR:	General Construction & Rainier Steel, JV
DRB COST:	$ 3,000; 4 DRB meetings, 0.04% of final cost
REFERENCES:	Owner: Oliver T. Harding, Seattle, WA
	Contractor: Jim Dick, Erik Reichelt, Seattle, WA
	DRB: Raymond J. Dodson, Woodside, CA
REMARKS:	The contractor completed the project one year early and earned the full early completion incentive bonus of $6.75 million. Aided by partnering and the presence of the DRB, the parties were able to resolve successfully several potential disputes that arose during this fast-paced project. The contract entailed over 170 change orders.
	The contractor utilized two graving docks, constructing four or five pontoons at one time. The specifications did not allow the placement of pontoons in the lake between October 15 and March 15 because of the possibility that wind storms would cause the new pontoons to damage the adjacent floating bridge.

Case History 7

PROJECT:	SR 405, NE 8TH STREET INTERCHANGE to NORTHRUP INTERCHANGE, Bellevue, WA
DESCRIPTION:	Construction of HOV lanes and 6 bridges and the widening of 13 existing bridges.

CONSTRUCTED:	1992–1994
PROVISIONS:	Generally followed 1989 ASCE DRB specification. Included partnering.
RECORD:	Disputes Heard:　2
	Recommendations Accepted:　0
	Disputes Litigated:　0
COSTS:	Estimate:　$32 million
	Bid:　$28 million
	Final:　$29 million
OWNER:	Washington State Department of Transportation
DESIGNER:	Washington State Department of Transportation
CONTRACTOR:	Kiewit Construction Company
DRB COST:	$40,000; 4 DRB meetings, 0.14% of final cost
REFERENCES:	Owner:　Philip A Fordyce, Seattle, WA
	Contractor:　Brett Harris, Seattle, WA
	DRB:　Theodore J. Trauner, Philadelphia, PA
REMARKS:	The contractor accelerated this 3-year project into 2 years. Although numerous problems arose during construction, the parties were able to resolve all the issues except the two disputes taken to the DRB.
	The parties participated in partnering, a new experience for both crews. Both parties agreed that partnering went well on the project, creating a better environment for communications, mutual trust, and joint problem solving.

Case History 8

PROJECT:	AMERICA WEST ARENA, Phoenix, AZ
DESCRIPTION:	Concert Hall and Phoenix Suns basketball arena. Seats 19,400. Steel frame roof is a two-way truss system. Bottom chord of the 330 feet long primary trusses were braced with 1.4 inch cable spreaders until truss was placed in tension on the ring beam. Construction schedule tight.
CONSTRUCTED:	1991–1993

PROVISIONS: AIA 201 (1987) General Conditions used. DRB
                       substituted for arbitration; 1989 ASCE DRB
                       specification used. Standby DRB was in place;
                       members did not receive progress reports. All
                       members were local.

RECORD: Disputes Heard: 0

                       Recommendations Accepted: 0

                       Disputes Litigated: 0

COSTS: Estimate: Not available

                       Bid: $47 million

                       Final: Not available

OWNER: City of Phoenix

DESIGNER: Ellerbe Becket Inc., Kansas City, KA

MANAGER: Huber, Hunt & Nichols, Phoenix, AZ

CONTRACTOR: Mardian Construction, Phoenix, AZ

DRB COST: $0

REFERENCES: Owner: Richard Mace, Phoenix, AZ

                       Contractor: Not available

                       DRB: Not available

REMARKS: Absence of disputes was attributed to having
                       a standby DRB in place. Attorney recommend-
                       ed that DRBs be included in all City of Phoenix
                       construction contracts. DRBs are currently in
                       place on contracts for the Central Library
                       and for a 450,000 square foot city office com-
                       plex.

Case History 9

PROJECT: INTER-ISLAND TERMINAL, HONOLULU
                       INTERNATIONAL AIRPORT, Honolulu, HI

DESCRIPTION: Fast-track construction schedule with airport
                       remaining fully operational at all times.

CONSTRUCTED: 1990–1993

PROVISIONS: Escrow bid documents and 1989 ASCE DRB
                       specified in addendum during bidding.

RECORD:	Disputes Heard: 2
	Recommendations Accepted: 2
	Disputes Litigated: 0
COSTS:	Bid: $119 million
	Final: $131 million
OWNER:	Hawaii Department of Transportation
DESIGNER:	Inter-Island Terminal Associates and MNS Associates, JV
CM:	KFC Airport Inc.
CONTRACTOR:	Kiewit-Pacific
DRB COST:	$50,000; 0.04% of final cost
REFERENCES:	CM: Brian Bowers, Honolulu, HI
	Contractor: Gordon Adkinson, Honolulu, HI
	DRB: Richard Elstner, Honolulu, HI
REMARKS:	Hawaii DOT director: "One of the greatest strengths of the DRB has been its deterrent value to help the owner, project manager, and contractor resolve problems at the lowest level." As a result of the success of this DRB, the owner now has a DRB on the adjacent project and recommends use on all future large projects.
	Escrow bid documents were key to settling several disputes. Information in the documents was used to convince the owner to allow the contractor to subcontract a portion of the work that had inadvertently been omitted from the bid form listing.

Case History 10

PROJECT:	305,000 SF OFFICE BUILDING COMPLEX, Alpharetta, GA
DESCRIPTION:	Two L-shaped buildings, one 4-story and one 3-story, with tenant fit-up, parking, and elegant landscaping.
CONSTRUCTED:	1991–1992

PROVISIONS: Followed 1989 ASCE DRB specification.
RECORD: Disputes Heard: 0
                     Disputes Litigated: 0
COSTS: Estimate: Not available
                     Bid: $12 million
                     Final: $19 million
OWNER: American Telephone & Telegraph Co.
DESIGNER: AT&T Real Estate Engineering Department
MANAGER: AT&T Real Estate Construction Department
CONTRACTOR: HCB Contractors
DRB COST: $7000; 0.04% of final cost
REFERENCES: Owner: Darryl McGehee, Atlanta, GA
                     Contractor: Christopher D. Gray, Atlanta, GA
                     DRB: L. Dennis Ballou, Esq., Atlanta, GA
REMARKS: Six prequalified bidders submitted fixed-price
                     bids. Four significant changes to the contract
                     were negotiated, increasing contract cost 60%
                     and time 40%.

                     First DRB meeting was held prior to selection
                     of chairman. All DRB members were residents
                     of Atlanta area. DRB met for half a day every 2
                     months. Monthly reports, including progress
                     photos, provided to DRB. Meetings informal,
                     without agenda or minutes.

                     Owner plans to use DRBs on all future con-
                     struction.

Case History 11

PROJECT: AKRON CONVENTION CENTER, Akron, OH
DESCRIPTION: Construction of 122,000 SF building with meet-
                     ing rooms and exposition hall.
CONSTRUCTED: 1992–1994
PROVISIONS: Verbatim 1991 ASCE DRB specification, except
                     modified to exclude disputes involving less
                     than $5000; for the American Subcontractors
                     Association to choose one member on behalf of
                     all the contractors; for owner to pay all costs of

regular DRB meetings; and for owner to determine which contractor is responsible for costs of dispute hearings and split that cost with contractor. Each contractor signed a separate TPA.

RECORD: Disputes Heard: 1

Recommendations Accepted: 1

Disputes Litigated: 0

COSTS: Estimate: $26 million

Bid: $19 million

Final: $ 21 million

OWNER: City of Akron

DESIGNER: URS Consultants, Cleveland, OH

CM: The Ruhlin Corporation, Akron, OH

CONTRACTOR: 19 prime contractors

DRB COST: $12,000; 0.06% of final cost

REFERENCES: Owner: Brad Beckert, Akron, OH

Contractor: American Subcontractors Association, Akron-Canton Chapter, John Dies, Akron, OH

CM: Tom Reynolds, Akron, OH

DRB: Ted Greive, Copley, OH

REMARKS: All DRB members resided in the Akron area; two were professional engineers retired from rubber companies; one was the former owner of an asphalt company.

The city of Akron is extremely pleased with the DRB. It will use the same DRB for its next contract, a parking structure for the Convention Center.

Guide Specification for Dispute Review Board

Introduction

This guide specification and its three-party agreement is a reformatted and revised version of the guide specification included in *Avoiding and Resolving Disputes During Construction* (ASCE, 1991). Several of the revisions are designed to strengthen the DRB process.

In the past, some provisions of the guide specification have been altered or have not been completely followed. This is particularly true of the following sections.

Specification 1.01 General

In several instances, the scope of DRB activities has been limited to specific types of issues or minimum or maximum claim values. There should be no limitation on the issues which can be referred to the board. To impose such limits invites controversy over those subjects and calls into question the commitment of the owner and the DRB concept itself.

Specification 1.02B Membership Criteria

The success of the DRB process is highly dependent on the stature of the board; criteria for membership must be exacting.

Neither party should hesitate to reject a proposed member if it has any concern regarding that individual's technical qualifications or neutrality. Parties sometimes hesitate to reject a potential board member because they do not wish to cause hard feelings at the start of the job. It is better to disagree on a board member than to accept a nominee who is not completely trusted.

The specification disqualifies most former employees of any party involved in the construction contract. This provision should be strictly observed. Consider the consequences of not following the provision. It will be very difficult for the other party to perceive the former employee as being completely neutral.

**Specification 1.02D
Selection Process**

Late or delayed organization of the DRB can be detrimental to the concept. Time-consuming selection and engagement procedures utilized by the owner or simple procrastination by either party is a frequent cause of delay.

A DRB organized after the onset of a dispute has reduced effectiveness.

**Specification 1.04 Review
of Disputes**

One of the important features of the DRB concept is the timely resolution of disputes. Some owners have impaired this feature by requiring time-consuming internal reviews or the preparation of completely documented submittals before the dispute can even be referred to the DRB. When legal policy requirements mandate a prior decision by an owner's designated representative, the process should be expedited.

DRB Guide Specification

1.01 General

A. Definitions

1. **Board**—See Dispute Review Board.

2. **Contract**—The Construction Contract of which this Specification section is a part.

3. **Dispute**—A claim, change order request, or other controversy that remains unresolved following good faith negotiations between authorized representatives of the Owner and Contractor.

4. **Dispute Review Board**—Three neutral individuals mutually selected by the Owner and Contractor to consider and recommend resolution of Disputes referred to it.

B. Summary

1. A Dispute Review Board will be established to assist in the resolution of Disputes in connection with, or arising out of, performance of the work of this Contract.

2. Either the Owner or the Contractor may refer a Dispute to the Board. Such referral should be initiated as soon as it appears that the normal Owner–Contractor dispute resolution effort is not succeeding, and prior to initiating other dispute resolution procedures or filing of litigation by either party.

3. Promptly thereafter, the Board will impartially consider the Dispute(s) referred to it. The Board will provide a nonbinding written recommendation for resolution of the Dispute to the Owner and the Contractor.

4. Although the recommendations of the Dispute Review Board should carry great weight for both the Owner and the Contractor, they are not binding on either party.

C. Scope

1. This specification describes the purpose, procedure, function, and features of the Dispute Review Board. A Three-Party Agreement among the Owner, Contractor, and three members using the form and content of Attachment A will formalize creation of the Board and establish the scope of its service and the rights and responsibilities of the parties. In the event of a conflict between this Specification and the Three-Party Agreement, the latter governs.

D. Purpose

1. The Board, as an independent third party, will assist in and
   facilitate the timely and equitable resolution of disputes
   between the Owner and the Contractor in an effort to avoid
   acrimony, construction delay, and more formal means of dispute resolution.

2. Creation of the Board is not intended to promote Owner or
   Contractor default on the responsibility of making a good-
   faith effort to settle amicably and fairly their differences by
   indiscriminate referral to the Board.

E. Continuance of Work

1. Both parties shall proceed diligently with the work and comply with all applicable Contract provisions while the Dispute
   Review Board considers a Dispute.

F. Tenure of Board

1. The Board will be deemed established after all parties execute
   the Three-Party Agreement.

2. The Board will be dissolved as of the date of final payment to
   the Contractor unless earlier terminated or dissolved by
   mutual agreement of the Owner and Contractor.

1.02   Membership

A. General

1. The Dispute Review Board will consist of one member nominated by the Owner and approved by the Contractor, one
   member nominated by the Contractor and approved by the
   Owner, and a third member nominated by the first two members and approved by both the Owner and the Contractor.
   The third member will serve as Chairman unless the parties
   otherwise agree.

B. Criteria

1. Experience

   a. It is desirable that all Dispute Review Board members be experienced with the type of construction involved in the project, interpretation of contract documents, and resolution of construction disputes.

   b. The goal in selecting the third member is to complement the experience of the first two and to provide leadership of the Board's activities.

2. Neutrality

   a. It is imperative that the Board members be neutral, act impartially, and be free of any conflict of interest.

   b. For purposes of this subparagraph, the term "member" also includes the member's current primary or full-time employer, and "involved" means having a contractual relationship with either party to the Contract, such as a subcontractor, architect, engineer, or construction manager.

   c. Prohibitions; disqualifying relationships for prospective members:

      (1) an ownership interest in any entity involved the construction contract, or a financial interest in the contract, except for payment for services on the Dispute Review Board;

      (2) previous employment by, or financial ties to, any party involved in the construction contract within a period of 30 years prior to award of the Contract, except for fee-based consulting services on other projects;

      (3) a close professional or personal relationship with any key member of any entity involved in the construction contract which, in the judgment of either party, could suggest partiality; or

      (4) prior involvement in the project of a nature which could compromise that member's ability to participate impartially in the Board's activities.

   d. Prohibitions; disqualifying relationships for members:

(1) employment, including fee-based consulting services, by any entity involved in the construction contract except with the express approval of both parties;

(2) discussion concerning, or the making of, an agreement with any entity involved in the Contract regarding employment after the Contract is completed.

C. Disclosure Statement

As a part of the selection process, the first two prospective members will be required to submit complete disclosure statements for the approval of both the Owner and the Contractor. Each statement shall include a résumé of experience, together with a declaration describing all past, present, and anticipated or planned future relationships, including indirect relationships through the prospective members' primary or full-time employer, to this project and with all parties involved in the Contract, including subcontractors, design professionals, and consultants. Disclosure of close professional or personal relationships with all key members of all parties to the Contract shall be included. The third Board member will be required to submit such a statement to the first two Board members and to the Owner and Contractor as a part of his selection and evaluation process..

D. Selection Process

1. Nomination and approval of first two members

   a. The Owner and the Contractor shall each nominate a proposed Board member and convey the nominee's name and disclosure statement to the other party within 4 weeks after Contract award.

   b. If the nominee is not rejected within 2 weeks after receipt of the name and disclosure statement, he shall be deemed approved.

   c. No reasons for rejection need be stated. In the event of rejection, the nominating party shall submit another nomination within 2 weeks of receipt of the notice of rejection. This process will be repeated until two mutually acceptable members are named.

2. Nomination and approval of third member

    a. Upon approval of both of the first two members, the Owner and the Contractor will notify them to begin selection of the third member. The first two members will endeavor to nominate a third member who meets all the criteria listed above. The third member shall be nominated within 4 weeks after the first two members are notified to proceed with his selection. The nominee's name and disclosure statement will be conveyed to the Owner and the Contractor, who will either accept or reject the nominee within four weeks. No reasons for rejection need be stated. In the event of rejection, the first two members will be requested to submit another nomination within two weeks of receipt of notice of rejection.

    b. In the event of an impasse in selection of the third member from nominees of the first two members, the third member shall be selected by mutual agreement of the Owner and the Contractor. In so doing, they may, but are not required to, consider nominees offered by the first two members.

E. Three-Party Agreement

1. All three Dispute Review Board members and the authorized representatives of the Owner and the Contractor shall execute the Dispute Review Board Three-Party Agreement (Attachment A) within 4 weeks after the selection of the third member.

1.03 Operation

A. General

1. Dispute Review Board operating procedures consistent with this specification will be formulated by the Board as a task under the Three-Party Agreement.

B. Contract Documents, Reports, and Information

1. The Owner will provide a conformed set of plans and specifications to each Board member.

2. The members will be kept informed of construction activity and other developments by means of timely transmittal of relevant information prepared by the Owner and the Contractor in the normal course of construction, including but not limited to periodic progress reports and minutes of progress meetings.

C. Periodic Meetings and Visits

1. The Board will visit the project site and meet with representatives of the Owner and the Contractor at regular intervals and at times of significant construction events. The frequency and scheduling of these visits will be as agreed among the Owner, the Contractor, and the Board, depending on the progress of the work. In the case of failure to agree, the Board will schedule the visits.

2. Each meeting shall consist of an informal roundtable discussion followed by a field observation of the work. The roundtable discussion will be attended by personnel of the Owner and the Contractor. The agenda will generally include the following:

   a. Meeting convened by the Chairman of the Dispute Review Board.

   b. Contractor discussion items:

      (1) work accomplished since the last meeting;

      (2) current status of the work schedule and schedule for future work;

      (3) anticipated or potential problems and proposed solutions;

      (4) status of current and potential disputes, claims, and other controversies.

   c. Owner discussion items:

      (1) the work schedule;

      (2) perspectives on potential disputes, claims, and other controversies;

      (3) status of past disputes, claims, and other controversies.

d. Such other items as the parties may wish to discuss with the Board.

e. Set tentative date for next meeting(s).

3. The Owner shall prepare minutes of regular meetings and circulate them for comments, revisions, and/or approval of all concerned.

4. The field observations shall cover all active segments of the work. The Board shall be accompanied by representatives of both the Owner and Contractor.

1.04   Review of Disputes

A. General

1. The Owner and the Contractor will cooperate to ensure that the Board considers Disputes promptly, taking into consideration the particular circumstances and the time required to prepare appropriate documentation.

2. Procedures and time periods may be modified by mutual agreement.

B. Prerequisites to Review

A Dispute is subject to referral to the Board when:

1. Either party believes that bilateral negotiations are not likely to succeed or have reached an impasse, and,

2. If the Contract provides for a prior decision by the [Architect] [Engineer] [Construction Manager], such a decision has been issued. (In this case the parties shall cooperate to timely comply with this requirement and may waive it by mutual agreement.)

C. Requesting Review

1. Either party may refer a dispute to the Board. Requests for Board review shall be submitted in writing to the Chairman of the Dispute Review Board and shall state the Dispute in connection with, or arising out of, performance of the work

of this Contract which the parties have considered but have been unable to resolve. The Request for Review shall state clearly and in full detail the specific issues of the Dispute to be considered by the Board and include a recommendation as to whether it may be heard at the next regular Board meeting or at a special meeting.

2. A copy of the Request for Review shall be simultaneously provided to the other party.

3. After conferring with both parties, the Board Chairman will establish a submittal schedule so that adequate time is allowed for the other party to respond to the requesting party's statement and for the Board members to review both statements and the supporting documentation before the hearing.

D. Scheduling Review

1. The Three-Party Agreement of Attachment A empowers the Board to schedule hearings.

2. Upon receipt of a Request for Review, the Chairman will schedule a hearing date.

E. Pre-hearing Requirements

1. Concise written position statements shall be prepared by both parties, with page number references to any supporting documentation, and submitted to each Board member and to the other party.

2. A single and complete compilation of supporting documentation, with pages consecutively numbered for ease of reference, is most desirable. The parties shall cooperate in compiling this documentation and submitting it to each Board member for review before the hearing.

3. The party requesting the Board review shall submit its position statement first, followed by the other party.

F. Hearing

1. Normally the hearing will be conducted at the job site. However, any location that would be more convenient and still provide all required facilities and access to necessary

documentation is satisfactory. Private sessions of the Board may be held at any convenient location.

2. The third member of the Board will act as Chairman of the hearing, or he may appoint one of the other members.

3. The Owner and the Contractor shall have representatives at all hearings. The Party requesting Board review will first present its position, followed by the other party. Each party will be allowed successive rebuttals until all aspects are fully covered. The Board members and the parties may ask questions, request clarification, or ask for additional data. In difficult or complex cases, additional hearings may be necessary in order to facilitate full consideration and understanding of all the evidence presented by both parties. Both the Owner and the Contractor shall be provided full and adequate opportunity to present all their evidence, documentation, and testimony regarding all issues before the Board.

4. Normally, a formal transcript will not be prepared. When requested by either party, the Board may allow recordation and transcription by a court reporter with the cost to be allocated as agreed by the parties. Audio or video recordings will not be permitted.

5. Attendance by, or participation of, lawyers will be at the discretion of the Board.

G. Deliberations

1. After the hearing is concluded, the Board will confer to formulate its recommendations. All Board deliberations shall be conducted in private, with all individual views kept strictly confidential from disclosure to others.

H. Recommendation

1. The Board's recommendation for resolution of the dispute will be provided in writing to both the Owner and the Contractor within 2 weeks of the completion of the hearings. In difficult or complex cases, and in consideration of the Board's schedule, this time may be extended by mutual agreement of all parties.

I. Acceptance or Rejection

1. Within 2 weeks of receiving the Board's recommendation, or such other time specified by the Board, both the Owner and the Contractor shall provide written notice to the other and to the Board of acceptance or rejection of the Board's recommendation. The failure of either party to respond within the specified period shall be deemed an acceptance of the Board's recommendation. If, with the aid of the Board's recommendation, the Owner and the Contractor are able to resolve their dispute, the Owner will promptly process any required Contract changes.

J. Clarification and Reconsideration

1. Should the dispute remain unresolved because of a bona fide lack of clear understanding of the recommendation, either party may request that the Board clarify specified portions of its recommendation.

2. If new evidence has become available, either party may request that the Board reconsider its recommendation.

K. Admissibility

1. If the Board's recommendation does not resolve the dispute, the written recommendation, including any minority report, will be admissible as evidence to the extent permitted by law in any subsequent dispute resolution proceeding or forum to establish (a) that a Dispute Review Board considered the Dispute, (b) the qualifications of the Board members, and (c) the Board's recommendation that resulted from the process.

1.05 Payment

A. The fees and expenses of all three members of the Board shall be shared equally by the Owner and the Contractor. The Contractor shall pay the invoices of all Board members after approval by both parties. The Contractor will then bill the Owner for 50 percent of such invoices.

B. The Owner, at its expense, will prepare and mail minutes and progress reports, and provide administrative services such as conference facilities and secretarial services.

C. If the Board desires special services such as legal or other consultation, accounting, data research, and the like, both parties must agree, and the costs will be shared by them as mutually agreed.

Attachment A to DRB Guide Specification

Dispute Review Board Three-Party Agreement

(To be executed after award of the Contract)

I. Parties

A. Owner: _____

B. Contractor: _____

C. Dispute Review Board Members:

1. _____

2. _____

3. _____

II. Situation

A. The Owner and Contractor are now engaged in the construction of the _____ (project name).

B. The _____ (project name) Contract provides for the establishment and operation of a Dispute Review Board ("Board") to assist in resolving Disputes as defined therein.

III. Purpose

A. The objective of the Board is to consider, fairly and impartially, the Disputes referred to it, and to provide written recommendations to the Owner and Contractor for resolution of these Disputes.

IV. Scope of Work

The scope of work of the Board includes, but is not limited to, the following:

A. Project Site Visits

1. The Board members shall visit the project site to keep abreast of construction activities and to become familiar with the work in progress. The frequency, time, and duration of these visits shall be mutually agreed upon among the Board, the Owner, and the Contractor. In case of failure to agree, the Board shall schedule the visits.

2. In the case of an actual or potential dispute involving an alleged differing site condition or specific construction problem, it may be advantageous for the Board to view personally any relevant conditions. If viewing by the Board would cause delay to the project, videos, photographs, and descriptions of these conditions, collected by either or both parties, will be utilized.

B. Establish Procedures

1. During its first meeting at the project site, the Board shall, with the agreement of all parties, establish procedures for the conduct of its routine site visits and its hearings of disputes. The conduct of its business shall, in general, be based on the Specification provisions.

2. It is not desirable to adopt hard-and-fast rules for the functioning of the Board. The entire procedure shall be kept flexible to adapt to changing situations. The Board shall initiate, with the Owner's and Contractor's concurrence, new procedures or modifications to old ones whenever this is deemed appropriate.

C. Recommend Resolution of Disputes

1. Upon receipt by the Board of a written Request for Review of a Dispute, either from the Owner or the Contractor, the Board shall convene a hearing to review and consider the Dispute and thereafter issue a written recommendation to the Owner and the Contractor.

2. It is expressly understood that all Board members are to act impartially and independently in the consideration of facts and conditions surrounding any dispute. During the hearing, no Board member shall express any opinion concerning the merit of any facet of the case.

3. The Board shall make every effort to reach a unanimous recommendation. If this proves impossible, the dissenting member may prepare a minority report.

4. The Board's recommendation, together with explanations of its reasoning, shall be submitted as a written report to both parties. The recommendation shall be based on the pertinent provisions of the Contract, applicable laws and regulations, and the facts and circumstances involved in the dispute. It is important for the Board to express, clearly and completely, the logic and reasoning leading to the recommendation so that both parties fully understand it.

5. The recommendation concerning any dispute is not binding, unless agreed otherwise by the Owner and the Contractor.

D. Other

1. The Board members shall become familiar with the Contract Documents, review periodic reports, and maintain a current file.

2. Except for providing the services required in the Agreement, the Board and its individual members shall refrain from giving any advice to either party concerning conduct of the work or the resolution of problems which might compromise the Board's integrity.

3. The Board shall perform services not specifically listed herein to the extent necessary to achieve the purpose of this Agreement.

V. Contractor Responsibilities

A. Except for its participation in the Board's activities as provided in the Contract Documents and in this Agreement, the Contractor shall not solicit advice or consultation from the Board or its members on matters dealing with the conduct of the work or resolution of problems which might compromise the Board's integrity.

B. The Contractor shall furnish each Board member with pertinent Contractor-prepared documents, such as progress
schedules, to supplement the documents provided by the
Owner.

VI. Owner Responsibilities

A. Except for its participation in the Board's activities as provided in the Contract Documents and in this Agreement, the
Owner shall not solicit advice or consultation from the Board
or its members on matters dealing with the conduct of the
work or resolution of problems which might compromise the
Board's integrity.

B. The Owner shall:

1. Furnish each Board member with one copy of all Contract
Documents, including but not limited to the specifications,
plans, addenda, progress schedule and updates, weekly
progress reports, minutes of progress meetings, change
orders, and other documents pertinent to the performance
of the contract and necessary to the Board's work.
2. In cooperation with the Contractor, coordinate the operations of the Board.
3. Furnish conference facilities at or near the site and provide
secretarial and copying services.

VII. Time for Beginning and Completion

A. The Board shall be active throughout the duration of the
Contract. It shall begin operation upon written authoriza-
tion of the Owner following execution of this Agreement
and shall terminate its activities on completion of the
Construction Contract after final payment has been made.

B. Except for choosing a third member by the first two members, the Board members shall not begin any work under the
terms of this Agreement until authorized in writing by the
Owner.

VIII. Payment

A. Payment for services of the Owner-appointed and Contractor-appointed members of the Board shall be at the rates agreed to between the Owner and the Contractor and the respective appointed Board members. Changes in the billing rates are subject to agreement between the Owner and the Contractor and the respective appointed members.

B. Payment for services rendered by the third member of the Board will be made at the rate agreed to among the Owner, the Contractor, and the third member. Changes in the billing rate are subject to agreement among the Owner, the Contractor, and the third member.

C. The first two members will be reimbursed for the time and expense associated with choosing the third member.

D. Direct, nonsalary expenses will be reimbursed at the actual cost to the Board member. These expenses may include, but are not limited to, automobile mileage, parking, and travel expenses from the Board member's point of departure to the initial point of arrival, automobile rental, food and lodging, printing, long-distance telephone, postage, and courier delivery. Billing for these expenses shall include an itemized listing supported by copies of the original bills, invoices, and expense accounts.

E. Each Board member may submit invoices for payment for work completed not more often than once per month during the progress of work. Such invoices shall be in a format approved by the Owner and Contractor, and accompanied by a general description of activities performed during that period. The value of work accomplished for payment shall be established from the billing rate and hours expended by the Board member together with direct, nonsalary expenses. Satisfactorily submitted invoices shall be paid within 30 days.

F. Invoices of the Board members shall be paid by the Contractor unless otherwise agreed by both parties and the Board. Payments shall constitute full compensation for work performed and services rendered and for all materials, supplies, and incidentals necessary to serve on the Board.

G. The cost records and accounts pertaining to this Agreement shall be kept available for inspection by representatives of the Owner or Contractor for 3 years after final payment.

IX. Termination of Agreement

A. This Agreement may be terminated by mutual agreement of the Owner and the Contractor at any time upon not less than 4 weeks' written notice to the other parties.

B. Board members may withdraw from the Board by providing 4 weeks' written notice. Board members may be terminated for or without cause only by their original appointer. Only the Owner may terminate the Owner-appointed member; only the Contractor may terminate the Contractor-appointed member; and the first two members or the Owner and Contractor must agree to terminate the third member.

C. Should the need arise to appoint a replacement Board member, the replacement member shall be appointed in the same manner as the original member was appointed. The selection of a replacement Board member shall begin promptly upon notification of the necessity and shall be completed within 4 weeks. This Agreement will be amended to indicate changes in Board membership.

X. Legal Relations

A. Each Board member, in the performance of his or her duties on the Board, is acting in the capacity of an independent agent and not as an employee of either the Owner or the Contractor.

B. The Owner and Contractor expressly acknowledge that each Board member is acting in a capacity intended to facilitate resolution of Disputes. Accordingly, it is agreed and acknowledged that to the fullest extent permitted by law, each Board member shall be accorded quasi-judicial immuni-

ty for any actions or decisions associated with the consideration, hearing, and recommendation of resolution for
Disputes rightfully referred to the Board.

C. Each Board member shall be held harmless for any personal
or professional liability arising from or related to Board
Activities. To the fullest extent permitted by law, the Owner
and Contractor shall indemnify all Board members for
claims, losses, demands, costs, and damages (including reasonable attorney's fees) for bodily injury, property damage,
or economic loss arising out of or related to Board members
carrying out Board functions. The foregoing indemnity is a
joint and several obligation.

D. Board members shall not assign any of the work of this
Agreement.

XI. Disputes Regarding This Three-Party Agreement

A. Disputes among the parties hereto arising out of this
Agreement which cannot be resolved by negotiation and
mutual concurrence between the parties and actions to
enforce any right or obligation under this Agreement shall
be initiated in the _____ Court of the
_____ (jurisdiction).

B. All questions shall be resolved by application of _____
_____ (jurisdiction) law.

C. The Board members hereby consent to the personal jurisdiction of the Court of the _____ (jurisdiction).

XII. Funding Agency Review

A. The _____ (Agencies funding the project)
have the right to review the recommendations and to attend
Board meetings and hearings, but not to attend private
Board deliberations.

XIII. Effective Date

A. This Agreement is effective as of _____,
_____.

Board Member   Board Member   Board Member

_____   _____   _____

Contractor   Owner

By: _____   By: _____

Title: _____   Title: _____

Sample Format of DRB Recommendation

Many different formats have been used successfully for DRB recommendations. The following general format is suggested as a good starting point for DRBs that are preparing their first recommendation. Additional formats are in the example recommendations of Appendix E.

Statement of Dispute and Positions

These first sections should, in a few sentences, identify and describe the dispute in summary form. A full discussion of the dispute history is not necessary.

Usually it is appropriate to present a simple statement of the two opposing positions of the owner and contractor.

In many cases, clear identification of the dispute and both parties' positions is a major step toward resolving the dispute.

Recommendation

The board's recommendation should be stated as clearly and simply as possible. In some cases, it may be helpful if the owner and contractor can agree between themselves, and request from the board, the content of the board's recommendation. For example, the parties might request that only merit be considered, or that workdays of delay be identified in specific categories.

Explanation of Recommendation

An explanation of the board's reasoning is given, so that the parties may understand how and why the DRB arrived at its recommendation. The immediate objective is to convince both parties that the board's recommendation is reasonable. The explanation is also provided for the benefit of possible later reviewers. This explanation is particularly necessary if the recommendation must be approved by the individuals who did not attend the hearing or by the owner's funding agencies. The explanation is also valuable in case the dispute goes on to another dispute resolution proceeding.

[Project Name]
Recommendation of Dispute Review Board

Dispute No. XX [NAME OF DISPUTE]

Hearing Date: _____ , 19xx

Dispute

Description of dispute. A one- or two-sentence summation of the dispute.

Contractor's Position

A short summation of the contractor's position as understood by the board.

Owner's Position

A short summation of the owner's position as understood by the board.

Recommendation

The board's specific recommendation for settlement of the dispute. (The recommended course is consistent with the explanation.)

Explanation

(This section could also be called Considerations, Rationale, Findings, Discussion, and so on.)

The board's description of how each recommendation was reached.

Respectfully submitted,

Date: _____   _____

Date: _____   _____

Date: _____   _____

Appendix $\mathbf{E}$

Examples of Dispute Review Board Recommendations

Introduction

The following two recommendations illustrate the product of dispute review boards. The recommendations were chosen to illustrate various types of disputes that are brought to DRBs. All the recommendations were unanimous and were signed by all members of the DRB. All recommendations were accepted by both parties.

None of these recommended quantum, but provided guidelines that allowed the owner and the contractor to negotiate the financial settlements of the claims. Note that all are fairly short. This is not always the case; recommendations on complex disputes have exceeded 100 pages. Recommendations on disputes that are not promptly brought to the DRB are also usually quite long.

San Antonio Tunnel

For details on this project, refer to the case history in Appendix B.

Since this was the Army Corps of Engineers' first DRB, its attorney (who had drafted the DRB specification) attended most of the meetings. The chairperson of this DRB was a civil engineer and construction attorney.

Sixteen disputes were originally submitted to the DRB. Two were presented in a written submission to the chairperson only; the contractor later withdrew both disputes. The contractor withdrew another dispute after presentation to the DRB. Of the 13 that were heard by the DRB, the owner asked for reconsideration of 2 recommendations. The DRB submitted additional reasoning and stood by its original recommendations in both cases.

Dispute No. 13 concerned complicated reinforcing steel in the elbow connecting the 24-foot-diameter tunnel to the 30-foot-diameter, 120-foot-deep outlet shaft. The recommendation partially favored the owner and partially the contractor. It included guidelines for quantum. On the basis of the recommendation, the parties successfully negotiated quantum and duration.

Recommendation

[The following is the verbatim text of the dispute review board recommendation for Dispute No. 13.]

Dispute No. 13—San Pedro Creek Tunnel Outlet Elbow Rebar

Dispute

Is the Contractor entitled to additional time, or compensation, or both for:

1. Furnishing and installing additional rebar required by plan omissions and Government additions to the plans?

2. Furnishing and installing additional rebar due to the Government requiring longer splice lengths?

3. Government delays in responding to requests for information and/or clarification of plans?

Contractor's Interpretation

1. The relevant plans were incomplete. The actual rebar required was approximately 508,000 lbs. more than was reasonably estimated at bid time.

2. Rebar splice lengths actually required were longer than could have been reasonably expected at bid time.

3. Slow Government response time and multiple design changes delayed completion of work more than the 18-day time extension granted in Mod P00058.

Government's Interpretation

1. Mod P00058 fully compensated the contractor for all additional rebar required by the Government.

2. ACI Class C rebar splices were required as specified. The specifications clearly stated that all splices shall be ACI Class C.

3. The Contractor was not delayed more than the 18 days granted by Mod P00058.

Recommendations

1. The plans did not show all necessary rebar and did not define a rebar layout that was practical to construct.

   The Contractor should be fully compensated for costs and time impact that can be shown to be caused by plan omissions and changes to the plans.

   The Board has been asked to not make specific recommendations regarding quantum, hence will not do so. However, the following general thoughts are offered for the consideration of the parties:

   a. Determination of quantum could logically be based on a comparison between reasonable cost and time or installation of the rebar actually used, relative to what would be anticipated from a reasonable interpretation of the plans at bid time. A detailed analysis of each of these two cases should be made.

   b. The quantum analysis should account for delays attributed to design changes and additions directed by the Government.

   c. The Contractor should be reimbursed for additional expenditures for detailing costs incurred due to the incomplete and inaccurate contract plans and those incurred as a result of the Government's revisions and additions.)

2. The Contractor is not entitled to additional compensation related to rebar splice length.

3. Whether or not the Contractor is entitled to delay time in excess of 18 days would require a detailed analysis of quantum, as described under Recommendation 1 above.

Explanation

1. The concrete and rebar of the lower elbow of the outlet structure is extremely complicated. The geometry of the outlet elbow differs from the inlet elbow in that a collar beam is provided within each end of the elbow, the invert is flattened, and a dewatering sump is added.

   The rebar as originally shown was not constructible; to correct this, layout of both the invert rebar and the arch rebar was revised. The sump was enlarged and rebar in the sump area, omitted from the original plans, was added. The invert rebar was also revised somewhat for the contractor's convenience.

   In addition, much of the elbow rebar was unusually difficult to place. During administration of the contract, the Government recognized the problems inherent in positioning this rebar and relaxed the specifications for variation of minimum concrete cover and of position.

   In summary, the exact nature of a desired, but practical rebar layout was not defined by the plans. This is evidenced by the changes in invert and arch rebar layout which evolved during detailed construction planning.

2. The Contract requirements for splice length could have been more clearly and directly stated—for example, in a manner such as that later used by the Government for Phase III work.

   However, the Board understanding is that a careful analysis of the specification requirement that "all splices shall be ACI Class C splices..." (Specification Section 3C, ¶7.4) would lead to the splice lengths actually required by the Government. This conclusion would be obtained either from the appropriate table in ACI 315 or from appropriate use of equations and criteria in ACI 318.

   Finally, no evidence was presented to indicate that the

Contractor's bid allowance for splices was in any way dependent upon any misunderstanding or confusion about interpretation of the Specification requirements for splices.

3. Mod P00058 acknowledged that Government redesign of the sump rebar caused some delay, and granted an 18-day time extension. Determination of whether or not this is an appropriate allowance would require a more detailed analysis of quantum, as described under Recommendation 1.

Bellevue Transit Access

The $19 million Bellevue Transit project was constructed for the Washington Department of Transportation by General Construction & 3A Industries, JV in 1991 and 1992. The project consisted of construction of an 1100-foot-long high-occupancy vehicle overpass through an extremely sensitive environmental area, plus bridge widening, retaining walls, mitigation ponds, and a major utility relocation.

The second of two disputes brought to the DRB concerned the use of nonapproved materials. Contract administration of this disputed issue was complicated. The utility company was responsible for inspection and payment of the utility relocation; the company was also responsible for paying for the relocation. The utility company had no contractual relation with the prime contractor; the utility relocation work was performed by a subcontractor that had no previous experience working with the utility company.

The DRB recommendation was accepted by all four parties: WashDOT, the utility company, General Construction, and the subcontractor.

Recommendation

[*The following is the verbatim text of the DRB's Recommendation.*]

Statement of Dispute

Did the Contractor's use of KOP-COAT Bitumastic 300-M coal tar epoxy comply with the Contract requirements for interior lining of the water-line fittings?

Analysis

The Dispute Review Board carefully reviewed the parties' presentations, the Contract Standard Specifications, and Special Provisions, and it relied on the following key factors in its deliberation in this matter.

The Contractor has a basic contractual obligation, per Section 1-06.1, Source of Supply and Quality of Material, of the Washington Department of Transportation Standard Specifications as follows:

> "All equipment, materials, and articles incorporated into the permanent work: Shall meet the requirements of the contract and be approved by the Engineer."

Recommendation

The Contractor failed to obtain written approval of the Engineer prior to installing permanent materials in the work. In accordance with Standard Specification Section 1-05.6, the Contractor shall bear the cost of replacement of unacceptable material. The Dispute Review Board recommends that the Contractor's claim be denied due to lack of entitlement.

Appendix **F**

Geotechnical Baseline Report

The traditional geotechnical design summary report (GDSR) is now referred to as a geotechnical baseline report (GBR). Although the GBR is not a vital part of the DRB process, it is an essential part of all contracts involving underground construction. An ASCE committee is currently preparing a new booklet, *Geotechnical Reports for Underground Construction*, which presents guidelines for the preparation of baseline reports, and the rationale for the name change to GBR.

The following is reproduced by permission from *Avoiding and Resolving Disputes During Construction*, copyright © 1991 by ASCE.

Introduction

The Geotechnical Baseline Report (GBR) sets forth the designer's anticipated subsurface conditions and their impact on design and construction. Thus the engineer and owner establish the geotechnical baseline for all anticipated conditions. Use of this single contractually established interpretation of conditions will generally result in more uniform bid prices, and less exposure to claims involving interpretation of subsurface data. It also fosters a cooperative climate, since the emphasis is on openness and candor.

If conditions are materially different from the baseline, and the contractor can demonstrate a financial impact, the contractor is entitled to additional compensation. Thus, the owner accepts the risk for conditions more difficult than the baseline.

Contractors can submit competitive bids on the basis of efficient management, innovative construction methods, and interpretation of conditions (with additional risk acceptance), knowing that the owner's geotechnical baseline will provide a clear basis for identifying differing conditions and limiting contractor exposure.

Description

The GBR should be included in the design engineer's scope of services as a required task to be accomplished in preparation of the contract documents.

The GBR, usually a separate document, is made part of the contract documents by inclusion. The specifications clearly state that in the event of apparent discrepancies or inconsistencies with other geotechnical data made available to the contractor, the GBR shall be given a higher order of precedence in reconciliation of the conflict.

It is suggested that a GBR be prepared for every construction contract involving a significant amount of work that is below the ground surface or that utilizes soil and rock materials. Examples include tunnels, buried pipelines, open or braced cuts, slurry walls, major fills, and complex deep foundations such as piles or drilled piers.

The GBR defines the geotechnical conditions assumed in the development of the design and in the preparation of the construction specifications. The GBR should contain a concise description of anticipated subsurface conditions and anticipated ground behavior consistent with construction methods likely to be used by the contractor. Where dewatering may be needed, an estimate of pumping quantities, well design, and well spacing should be included. Estimates should be made of other key factors such as anticipated drilling conditions, slope stability, support requirements, and water inflows. These estimates will be used as the basis for identifying potential differing site conditions and must therefore be as realistic as practical, clearly defining the extent of work anticipated.

Use of imprecise and vague language must be avoided. For example, when the engineer says something "may" occur, it is not unreasonable for the contractor to assume it "may not" occur. A dispute can easily arise from such wording.

The GBR should contain an explanation of the contract bid item quantities which are closely related to geologic features, so that bidders may better understand the intent of the contract documents and may prepare more responsive bids. Discrepancies between the GBR and other contract documents must be eliminated.

The GBR should be specific and brief. To accomplish the objective of the GBR, it is recommended that the report contain at least the following major sections:

Geologic Setting

Geologic Features of Engineering and Construction Significance

Man-made Features of Engineering and Construction Significance

Anticipated Ground Behavior and Construction Difficulties

Influence on Final Design Features

Influence on Contract Plans and Specifications

Discussion

Some owners have expressed concerns over the GBR in the fear that the geotechnical baseline could be incorrect. For example, if the baseline is overly conservative, bid prices are likely to be higher. On the other hand, if the baseline is overly optimistic, exposure to claims and cost overruns is increased.

Key to using the GBR is the owner's appreciation of how it affects the management of risk. Overall risk is inversely proportional to the extent of subsurface investigations, and to the expertise and level of effort the engineer applies to the design and preparation of contract documents. A more conservative geotechnical baseline will reduce the risk of unexpected cost increases, but will increase the contract price. The owner, with the advice and cooperation of the engineer, has considerable control over these trade-offs.

The engineer, having months to assess the conditions and develop an appropriate interpretation, is in the best position to assess the reliability and accuracy of the available data. The contractor, on the other hand, has only weeks to assimilate all the available data and develop a bid.

Nothing can eliminate the risk of encountering differing site conditions. But the potential for costly disputes and possible litigation over what constitutes differing conditions is greatly reduced, if not eliminated, with well-defined geotechnical baselines. Further, the owner does not pay in advance for contractor contingencies, and then pay again when a claim results from an apparent differing site condition. The contractor is also protected by having a well-defined basis for preparing a bid and a clear definition of the limits of exposure.

When the geotechnical baseline is not well defined, the low bidder often is overly optimistic, does not fully appreciate the complexity of the work, and submits an unrealistic bid. The common result is an extensive series of claims as the contractor attempts to recover the losses. This problem can be reduced with a well-written GBR.

When properly prepared, the GBR enhances the contractor's opportunity to be innovative. By having the anticipated ground behavior identified for commonly used construction methods and procedures, the contractor can more readily anticipate the potential impact of innovative methods. The project can then be bid on and constructed using innovative methods, provided the contractor is willing to assume the added risks involved.

Owners have has also expressed concern over potential increases in the engineer's professional liability when faced with the added task of setting the geotechnical baseline. In fact, the opposite is the case. The GBR is not a guarantee, but is the informed judgment of a competent professional. When properly developed, the GBR presents realistic baseline conditions and ground behavior which the contractor may rely on in preparing a bid. Professional liability risks are reduced accordingly.

Experience

The thorough geotechnical assessment of design and construction considerations required to develop the GBR results in better geotechnical documents than does the presentation of factual data alone, with little or no interpretation. Many claims (and resulting settlements) have been based on one or two words, included (or omitted) on boring log descriptions, that the contractor has subsequently maintained were key in bid preparation. A clear, specific statement of the conditions to be assumed during bid preparation will facilitate resolution of disputes in a more timely and cost-effective manner for both owner and contractor.

Since GBR reports were introduced into Washington Metropolitan Area Transit Authority (WMATA) tunnel work, the number of differing site condition claims, and subsequent amount of financial awards, has decreased significantly. WMATA and its contractors have been able to settle most claims using the GBR at the contracting officer's level. The concept has received wide acceptance by all the tunnel designers engaged by WMATA. Contractors have expressed the opinion that it is beneficial in bidding on the job and planning the work.

Many other owners have incorporated GBRs in one form or another in their construction projects. They include:

Alaska Power Authority

City and County of Honolulu

City of Los Angeles

Colorado Department of Highways

Hawaii Department of Transportation

Massachusetts Water Resources Authority

Milwaukee Metropolitan Sewerage District

Municipality of Anchorage

Municipality of Metropolitan Seattle

Pennsylvania Turnpike Commission

Pierce County (Washington) Public Works Department

Rail Construction Corporation, Los Angeles

U.S. Bureau of Reclamation

Washington State Department of Transportation

Washington (D.C.) Suburban Sanitary Commission

Reports from owners, engineers, and contractors involved in projects that employ a GBR have been consistently favorable. Some have credited the GBR directly with saving millions of dollars in avoided claims and litigation.

Appendix **G**

Escrow Bid Documents

The following specification has been slightly revised from the 1991 ASCE/UTRC version. It was written, reviewed, and endorsed by attorneys with extensive experience in the DRB process. The specification should be included in the Special Provisions or Supplementary Conditions section of the Contract Documents and noted in the Instructions to Bidders. (Choices are enclosed in parenthesis in Section 5, of this specification.) Revisions to the specification can seriously dilute the effectiveness of escrow bid documents.

A bid document certification form accompanies the specification.

The following is reproduced by permission from *Avoiding and Resolving Contract Disputes During Construction*, copyright © 1991 by ASCE.

Escrow Bid Document Specification

1. Scope

The three low bidders shall submit, within the specified time after receipt of bids, one copy of all documentary information generated in preparation of bid prices for this project. This material is hereinafter referred to as Escrow Bid Documents. The Escrow Bid Documents of the successful bidder will be held in escrow for the duration of the contract.

The successful bidder agrees, as a condition of award of the contract, that the Escrow Bid Documents constitute the only complete documentary information used in preparation of his bid. No other bid preparation information shall be considered in resolving disputes.

Nothing in the Escrow Bid Documents shall change or modify the terms or conditions of the Contract Documents.

2. Ownership

The Escrow Bid Documents are, and shall always remain, the property of the contractor, subject only to joint review by the owner and the contractor, as provided herein.

The owner stipulates and expressly acknowledges that the Escrow Bid Documents, as defined herein, constitute trade secrets. This acknowledgment is based on the owner's express understanding that the information contained in the Escrow Bid Documents is not known outside the bidder's business, is known only to a limited extent and only by a limited number of employees of the bidder, is safeguarded while in bidder's possession, is extremely valuable to bidder, and could be extremely valuable to bidder's competitors by virtue of it reflecting bidder's contemplated techniques of construction.

Owner acknowledges that the bidder expended substantial sums of money in developing the information included in the Escrow Bid Documents and further acknowledges that it would be difficult for a competitor to replicate the information contained therein. Owner further acknowledges that the Escrow Bid Documents and the information contained therein are made available to owner only because such action is an express prerequisite to award of the contract. Owner further acknowledges that the Escrow Bid Documents include a compilation of information used in the bidder's business, intended to give the bidder an opportunity to obtain an advantage over competitors who do not know of or use the contents of the documentation.

Owner agrees to safeguard the Escrow Bid Documents, and all information contained therein, against disclosure to the fullest extent permitted by law.

3. Purpose

Escrow Bid Documents will be used to assist in the negotiation of price adjustments and change orders and in the settlement of disputes, claims and other controversies. They will not be used for preaward evaluation of the contractor's anticipated methods of construction or to assess the contractor's qualifications for performing the work.

4. Format and Contents

Bidders may submit Escrow Bid Documents in their usual cost-estimating format. It is not the intention of this specification to cause the bidder extra work during the preparation of the proposal, but to ensure that the Escrow Bid Documents will be adequate to enable complete understanding and proper interpretation for their intended use. The Escrow Bid Documents shall be in the language of the specifications.

It is required that the Escrow Bid Documents clearly itemize the estimated costs of performing the work of each bid item contained in the bid schedule. Bid items should be separated into subitems as required to present a complete and detailed cost estimate and allow a detailed cost review. The Escrow Bid Documents shall include all quantity takeoffs, crew, equipment, calculations of rates of production and progress, copies of quotations from equipment manufacturers, subcontractors and suppliers, and memoranda, narratives, consultant's reports, add/deduct sheets, and all other information used by the bidder to arrive at the prices contained in the bid proposal. Estimated costs should be broken down into the bidder's usual estimate categories such as direct labor, repair labor, equipment operation, equipment ownership, expendable materials, permanent materials, and subcontract cost as appropriate. Plant and equipment and indirect costs should be detailed in the bidder's usual format. The contractor's allocation of plant and equipment, indirect costs, contingencies, markup, and other items to each bid item shall be included.

All costs shall be identified. For bid items amounting to less than $10,000, estimated unit costs are acceptable without a detailed cost estimate, providing that labor, equipment, materials, and subcontracts, as applicable, are included and provided that indirect costs, contingencies, and markup, as applicable, are allocated.

Bid documents provided by the owner should not be included in the Escrow Bid Documents unless needed to comply with the requirements of this specification.

5. Submittal

The Escrow Bid Documents shall be submitted by the three lowest bidders in a sealed container within (24, 48, 72) hours after the time of receipt of bids. The container shall be clearly marked on the outside with the bidder's name, date of submittal, project name and the words "Escrow Bid Documents."

The Escrow Bid Documents shall be accompanied with the Bid Documentation Certification, signed by an individual authorized by the bidder to execute the bidding proposal, stating that the material in the Escrow Documentation constitutes the complete, only, and all documentary information used in preparation of the bid and that he or she has personally examined the contents of the Escrow Bid Documents container and has found that the documents in the container are complete.

Prior to award, Escrow Bid Documents of the apparent successful bidder will be unsealed, examined, organized, and inventoried by representatives of the owner, together with members of the contractor's staff who are knowledgeable in how the bid was prepared.

This examination is to ensure that the Escrow Bid Documents are authentic, legible, and complete. It will not include review of, and will not constitute approval of, proposed construction methods, estimating assumptions, or interpretations of Contract Documents. This examination is subject to the condition that, as trade secrets, the Escrow Bid Documents are proprietary and confidential as described in Section 2. Examination will not alter any condition(s) or term(s) of the contract.

If all the documentation required in Section 4, "Format and Contents," has not been included in the original submittal, additional documentation shall be submitted, at the owner's discretion, prior to award of the contract. The detailed breakdown of estimated costs shall be reconciled and revised, if appropriate, by agreement between the contractor and the owner before making the award.

If the contract is not awarded to the apparent successful bidder, the Escrow Bid Documents of the bidder next to be considered for award shall be processed as described above.

Timely submission of complete Escrow Bid Documents is an essential element of the bidder's responsibility and a prerequisite to contract award. Failure to provide the necessary Escrow Bid Documents will be sufficient cause for the owner to reject the bid.

If the bidder's proposal is based on subcontracting any part of the work, each subcontractor, whose total subcontract price exceeds 5 percent of the total contract price proposed by the bidder, shall provide separate Escrow Bid Documents to be included with those of the bidder. These documents will be opened and examined in the same manner and at the same time as the examination described above for the apparent successful bidder.

If the contractor wishes to subcontract any portion of the work after award, the owner retains the right to require the contractor to submit Escrow Bid Documents from the subcontractor before the subcontract is approved.

Escrow Bid Documents submitted by unsuccessful bidders will be returned unopened, unless opened as provided above, as soon as they are no longer needed by the owner and no later than immediately following award of the contract.

6. Storage

The Escrow Bid Documents of the successful bidder will be placed in escrow prior to award of the contract, for the life of the contract, in a mutually agreeable institution. The cost of storage will be paid by the owner.

7. Examination After Award of Contract

The Escrow Bid Documents shall be examined by both the owner and the contractor, at any time deemed necessary after award of the contract by either the owner or the contractor, to assist in the negotiation of price adjustments and change orders, or the settlement of disputes.

Examination of the Escrow Bid Documents after award of the contract is subject to the following conditions:

a. As trade secrets, the Escrow Bid Documents are proprietary and confidential as described in Section 2.

b. The owner and the contractor shall each designate, in writing to the other party and a minimum of 10 days prior to examination, representatives who are authorized to examine the Escrow Bid Documents. With the consent of both the owner and contractor, members of the Dispute Review Board may examine the Escrow Bid Documents if required to assist in the settlement of a dispute. No other person shall have access to the Escrow Bid Documents.

c. Access to the Escrow Bid Documents will take place only in the presence of duly designated representatives of both the owner and contractor.

8. Final Disposition

The Escrow Bid Documents will be returned to the contractor at such time as the contract has been completed and final settlement has been achieved.

Bid Document Certification

The undersigned hereby certifies that the bid documentation contained herein constitutes the complete, only and all documentary information used in preparation of the bid and that I have personally examined these contents and have found that this bid documentation is complete.

By: _____

Title: _____

Firm: _____

Date: _____

Bibliography

In general, references 1 through 25 are reproduced from *Avoiding and Resolving Disputes During Construction*, (ASCE, 1991).

1. American Society of Civil Engineers (ASCE), *Construction Risks and Liability Sharing.* Conference Proceedings, Vols. I and II, 1980.
2. ASCE. *Avoiding and Resolving Disputes in Underground Construction,* 1989.
3. Associated General Contractors of America. *Owner's Guide to Saving Money by Risk Allocation.* Washington, D.C., 1990.
4. Association of Engineering Firms Practicing in the Geosciences. *Alternative Dispute Resolution for the Construction Industry,* 1988.
5. Building Research Advisory Board. *Exploratory Study on Responsibility, Liability, and Accountability for Risks in Construction.* Washington, D.C.: National Academy of Sciences, 1978.
6. "Caltrans Sets Up Dispute Board," *ENR,* March 29, 1990, pp. 28–30.
7. Coffee, John D. "Dispute Review Boards in Washington State," *Arbitration Journal,* Vol. 43, No. 4 (December 1988).
8. "Hope for Tunneling Disputes," *ENR,* October 29, 1987, p. 14.
9. King, B. Palmer. "Arbitration—The Colorado Innovation." Presented to the American Society of Soils and Foundation Engineers, Lake of the Ozarks, MO, October 1980.
10. Kuesel, Thomas R. *Improving Contracting Methods—the Engineer's Viewpoint.* Proceedings of the 1983 Rapid Excavation and Tunneling Conference.
11. McOllough, P. R. *Eisenhower Memorial Tunnel—How Colorado Department of Highways Improved Contracting Practices and Management.* Proceedings of the 1981 Rapid Excavation and Tunneling Conference.

12. McOllough, P. R. "Contractual Requirements and Design, Eisenhower Memorial Tunnel, Second Bore," *Transportation Research Record*, No. 792 (1981), pp. 14–19.

13. Parker, Harvey. "Concept and Construction of the Mt. Baker Ridge Tunnel," *Tunnels & Tunnelling*, March 1990, pp. 57, 58.

14. Poulsen, H. R., Jr. "Minimizing Adversary Contractual Relationships for the Eisenhower Memorial Tunnel, Second Bore," *Transportation Research Record*, No. 792 (1981), pp. 19–23.

15. Shanley, E. M., "A Better Way," *Civil Engineering*, December 1989, pp. 58–59.

16. Siccardi, A. J. "Minimizing Potential for Adversary Contractual Relationships During Construction of Eisenhower Memorial Tunnel," *Transportation Research Record*, No. 792 (1981), pp. 23–32.

17. "Tunnel Risk Sharing," *ENR*, April 15, 1982, p. 76.

18. Underground Technology Research Council's Technical Committee on Tunnel Lining Design. *Guidelines for Tunnel Lining Design*, T. D. O'Rourke, ed. New York: ASCE, 1984.

19. U.S. National Committee on Tunneling Technology (USNCTT). *Better Contracting for Underground Construction*. Washington, D.C.: National Academy of Sciences, 1974. Reprinted as Report No. DOT-TST-76-48, U.S. Department of Transportation.

20. USNCTT. *Better Management of Major Underground Construction Projects*. Washington, D.C.: National Academy of Sciences, 1978.

21. USNCTT. *Executive Presentation: Recommendations for Better Management of Major Underground Construction Projects*. Washington, D.C.: National Academy of Sciences, 1978.

22. USNCTT. *Executive Presentation: Recommendations on Better Contracting for Underground Construction*. Washington, D.C.: National Academy of Sciences, 1976.

23. USNCTT. *Geotechnical Site Investigations for Underground Projects*. Two volumes. Washington, D.C.: National Academy of Sciences, 1984.

24. USNCTT Subcommittee on Contracting Practices for the Superconducting Super Collider. *Contracting Practices for the Underground Construction of the Superconducting Super Collider*. Washington, D.C.: National Academy of Sciences, 1989.

25. Washington State Department of Transportation. *Mt. Baker Ridge Tunnel: World's Largest Diameter Soft-Earth Tunnel*, undated.

Most of the following additional references were published since the 1991 edition of *Avoiding and Resolving Disputes During Construction* (ASCE).

26. Allen, Richard K. *Dispute Avoidance and Resolution.* New York: ASCE, 1993.

27. American Arbitration Association. *Construction Industry Dispute Review Board Procedures,* 1993.

28. Arrigoni, Gianni Alberto. "Better Risk Management Through Dispute Review Board," *Gallerie e Grandi Opere Sotterranee,* July and November 1993.

29. "ASCE Document Is Model for New Procedures Promulgated by Arbitration Group," *ASCE News,* July 1993.

30. Battelle, Anthony E., and Kurt L. Dettmen. *Alternate Dispute Resolution at Boston's Central Artery/Tunnel: A Comparison with the Classic UTRC DRB Concept.* Presented at Construction Superconference, San Francisco, November 12, 1993.

31. Carr, Frank; Rubin, Robert A.; and Robert J. Smith. *Dispute Review Boards,* Construction Law Update, Ch. 5. New York: Wiley, 1992.

32. Center for Public Resources. "Preventing and Resolving Construction Disputes," Ch. 6 in *Jobsite Dispute Resolution,* 1991.

33. Denning, James. "More Than an Underground Success," *Civil Engineering,* December 1993, pp. 42–45.

34. Diekmann, James E.; Girard, Matthew J.; and Nader Abdul-Hadi. *DPI—Disputes Potential Index: A Study into the Predictability of Contract Disputes.* A Report to the Construction Industry Institute, 1994.

35. DPIC Companies. *A New Look at Loss Prevention,* 1991.

36. "Escrowing May Be Heading to California's Highways," *ENR,* December 21, 1992, p. 8.

37. Groton, James P. *Dispute Review Boards—Backdoor Partnering.* Presented at Construction Leadership Conference, March 1993: Reprinted in *Constructor,* November 1993, p. 22.

38. Huse, Joseph. "Alternative Dispute Resolution in Tunnel Project," *Tunnels & Tunnelling,* November 1992, pp. 44–46.

39. Jaynes, Gordon L. "Disputes Review Boards—Yes!" *International Construction Law Review,* 1993.

40. Jones, Donald W. *Disputes Review Boards: Their Place Within the Building Construction Industry.* Thesis, State University, State College, PA, 1992.

41. Jones, Donald W., and Victor E. Sanvido. "Dispute Review Boards and Vertical Construction," *Construction Business Review,* November–December 1992.

42. Josephson, Robert A. *The Good News About Claims.* Report presented to the American Association of State Highway Officials, 1992.

43. Kane, Christopher. "Mitigating Construction Disputes," *Public Utilities Fortnightly,* July 1, 1992.

44. Kane, Christopher. *Building Effective Contractual Relationships for Power Projects.* Presented to 5th International Conference and Exhibition for the Power Generating Industries, Orlando, FL, November 17–19, 1992.

45. Kellogg, Joseph C. "The Rapid Response Team and Disputes Review Board Concept; A Form of Alternative Dispute Resolution," *KC-News,* September 1990.

46. Kohnke, John R. "Dispute Review Boards, Rising Star of Construction ADR," *Arbitration Journal,* June 1993.

47. "Like It or Not, Change Is on the Way for Firms," *ENR,* November 16, 1992.

48. Muller, Frank. "Don't Litigate. NEGOTIATE," *Civil Engineering,* December 1990, pp. 66–68.

49. Muller, Frank. "Dispute Review Boards Are Worthwhile," *Civil Engineering News,* January 1991, p. 4.

50. Parvin, Cordell. "Review Boards Need No Lawyers," *Roads and Bridges,* June 1991.

51. Pike, Andrew. "Disputes Review Boards and Adjudicators," *International Construction Law Review,* April 1992, pp. 157–171.

52. Poirot, James W. "Alternative Dispute Resolution Techniques: Design Professional's Perspective," *ASCE Journal of Performance of Constructed Facilities,* Vol. 1, No. 4 (November 1987).

53. "Review Boards Gaining," *ENR,* April 29, 1991, pp. 22, 23.

54. Roy, Richard J. "In ADR, DRBs Proving A-OK," *Constructor,* May 1992, pp. 58, 59.

55. Smith, John A. "How to Use Dispute Review Boards for Claims Settlement During Contracts," *Cost Engineering,* August 1993. (Note that this article appears to endorse the use of DRBs after completion of construction. This is not an effective use of the DRB concept.)

56. Smith, Robert J. *Dispute Review Boards—Using the ASCE Model: If It's Not Broken, Don't Fix It.* Presented at Annual Meeting, Section of Public Contract Law, American Bar Association, New York, August 9, 1993.

57. Smith, Robert J. "Dispute Review Boards for Tunnelling Projects Using the ASCE Model," *Tunnelling and Underground Space,* Vol. 9, No. 1 (1994).

58. "U.S. Tunnels Contract Keeps Down Legal Bills," *New Civil Engineer* (London), November 28, 1991, p. 6.

59. Vorster, M. C. *Dispute Resolution and Prevention: Alternative Dispute Resolution in Construction with Emphasis on Dispute Review Boards.* Report to the Construction Industry Institute, 1993.

60. Weston, David C., and G. Edward Gibson. "Partnering Project Performance in U.S. Army Corps of Engineers," *ASCE Journal of Management on Engineering,* Vol. 9, October 1993.

Index

Adjudicator, 27, 67
Admissibility, 38
ADR (alternative dispute resolution), 15, 67–68
AGC (Associated General Contractors of America), 11, 16
Akron, city of, 88, 118
Alternative dispute resolution (ADR), 15
America West Arena case history, 115
American Arbitration Association (AAA), 16, 35
  DRB procedures, 35
American Telephone and Telegraph, 88
American Underground Association, 16, 117
Anchorage, city of, 88, 155
Annex A of Conditions of Particular Application, 78–86
Appointment of members, 68
ASCE (American Society of Civil Engineers), 1
  DRBs, 32, 34
Associated General Contractors of America (AGC), 11, 16
Attorney's perspective, 38
Avoiding and Resolving Disputes During Construction, 1, 36
Avoiding and Resolving Disputes in Underground Construction, 1, 36

Bangladesh, 88
Barriers, perceived, 27–32
BART (San Francisco Bay Area Rapid Transit), 14
Bellevue (Washington) projects, 111–112, 114–115, 149–150
Benefits, 21, 25–26
Better Contracting for Underground Construction, 9
Bid prices, 36
Blocking attempts, 73–74

Boundary Dam, State of Washington, 8–9
Bradley Lake project, 108–109

California Department of Transportation, 14
Case histories, 107–119
Central Artery and Tunnel, Massachusetts Highway Department, 14
Chambers Creek Tunnel (Tacoma, Washington), 10
Channel Tunnel, 12, 33
CII (Construction Industry Institute), 2, 22–25
Clause 67, FIDIC, 64–67, 75–78
Colorado, University of, 15
Colorado Department of Highways, 10, 155
Compensation of members, 70–71, 80–81
Conditions of Contract (International), 64
Conditions of Particular Application, 75–86
  Annex A, 78–86
Construction Industry Dispute Avoidance and Resolution Task Force, 16
Construction Industry Institute (CII), 2, 6, 15, 16
Construction Industry Presidents Forum, 16
Consulting advice, 40
Contra Costa County, 88
Contractor's perspective, 37–38
Costs of the DRB, 6–7, 71
CPR Institute for Dispute Resolution, 16
Cross-examination, 32

Declaration of Acceptance, 75, 86
Deliberation, 59–60
Development of the DRB concept, 7–17
Diekmann, James (Professor), 15

About the Authors

ROBERT M.MATYAS is a construction management consultant and retired vice president for facilities and business operations at Cornell University. He was chairman of the Task Committee on Dispute Review Boards of the ASCE.

A. A. MATHEWS is a construction engineering consultant specializing in feasibility, design, construction, and contractual problems on dams, tunnels, and other large civil engineering projects.

ROBERT J. SMITH is a practicing attorney and a principal of Construction Strategies, Inc., a subsidiary of Wickwire Gavin, P.C., providing dispute avoidance, dispute resolution, and contract review services.

P. E. SPERRY is a construction consultant with more than 30 years of experience in tunnel construction. He is a member and former chairman of the Underground Technology Research Council of the ASCE.